Apples On Parade
Winchester and Fredrick County, Virginia

around town CAROUSELS abound
Meridian, Mississippi

Art and S

Colorado Springs, Colorado

BLACKSTONE VALLEY CANOE TRAIL
Pawtucket, Rhode Island

CAROUSEL HORSES ON PARADE
Myrtle Beach, South Carolina

Cat'n Around Downtown
Racine, Wisconsin

COOL KIDDIE CARS
Elmhurst, Illinois

Corn-on -the-Curb
Bloomington, Illinois

CRANES ON PARADE
Kearney, Nebraska

STAMPEDE
Custer, South Dakota

DOGHOUSE DAYS OF SUMMER
St. Paul, Minnesota

DOGNY®
New York City, New York

Dolphins BY DESIGN
Indianapolis, Indiana

Dolphins on Parade™
Key West, Florida

Fish Out of Water
Baltimore, Maryland

Frogs • Fur • Friends
Grosse Pointe, Michigan

Galaxy of Stars
Connecticut

gaLLopaLooza
LOUSIVILLE'S SIDEWALK DERBY
Louisville, Kentucky

GRANTS PASS "BEARFEST"
Grants Pass, Oregon

GUITAR MANIA®
Cleveland, Ohio

Hands Across Eau Claire
Eau Claire, Wisconsin

HEARTS IN SAN FRANCISCO
San Francisco, California

Lions on Safari
Sacramento, California

Llamas of Lludlow
Ludlow, Vermont

LOOKING FOR LUCY
St. Paul, Minnesota

Magical Giving Garden; Farmyard Friends
Naperville, Illinois

Overalls All Over
"An American Gothic Happening"
Cedar Rapids, Iowa

Pandamania
Washington, DC

Party Animals
Washington, DC

Path of the Bighorn®
Palm Springs, California

PIGS ON PARADE
Seattle, Washington

PLAINVIEW CATTLE DRIVE
Plainview, Texas

Prairie Dog Quest
Sioux City, Iowa

PUMAS on PARADE
Durango, Colorado

SPIRIT OF THE BUFFALO
Oklahoma City, Oklahoma

The Summer of Labs
Sun Valley, Idaho

THESE BOOTS are made for TALKING
Cheyenne, Wyoming

THE TRAIL OF PAINTED PONIES
Santa Fe, New Mexico
Carefree, Arizona

THE UTAH BUFFALO ROUND-UP
Utah

We Let The Dawgs Out
Athens, Georgia

Wild Salmon on Parade
Anchorage, Alaska

Wilmington Wonderland
Wilmington, Delaware

WHEN PIGS FLEW, GUITARS ROCKED
AND COWS JUMPED OVER THE MOON

Nancy -
Here's to the Merry Duckster memories!
Linda [illegible]
2008

www.AmericanArtParades.com

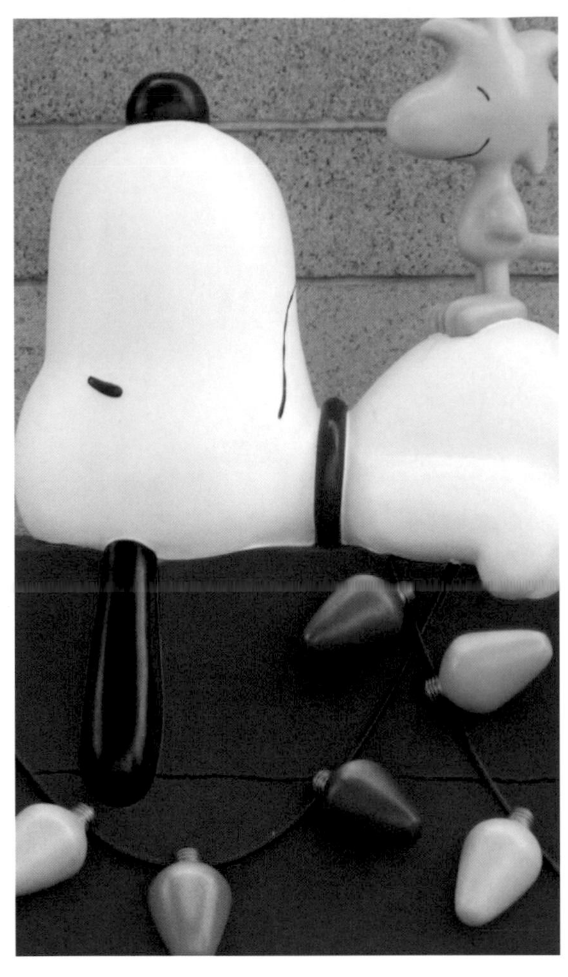

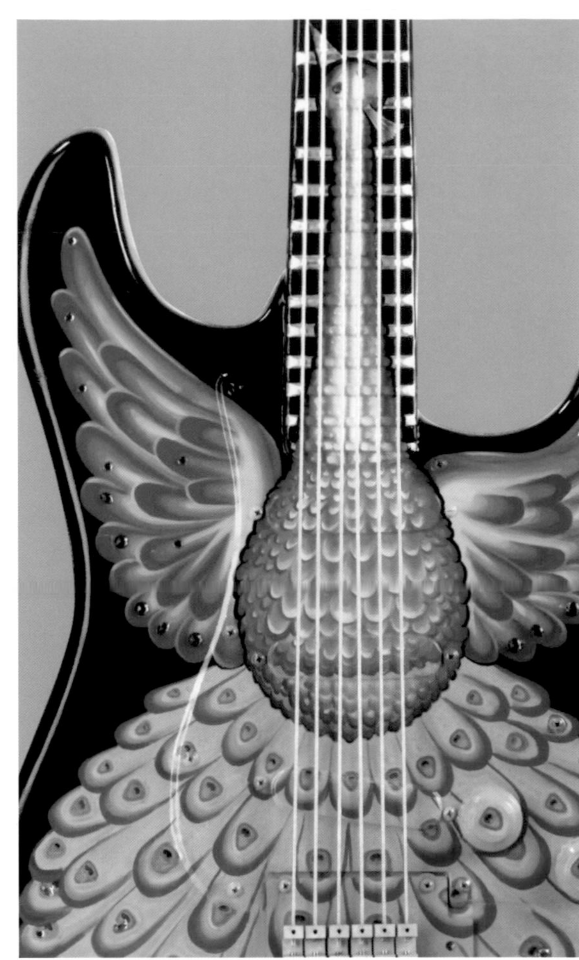

www.AmericanArtParades.com

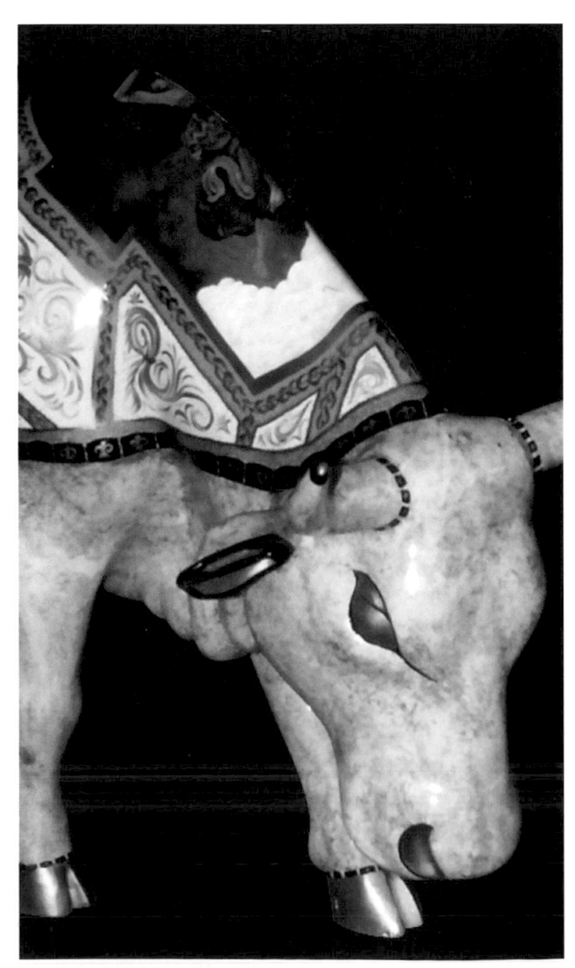

AMERICAN ART PARADES

WHEN PIGS FLEW, GUITARS ROCKED AND COWS JUMPED OVER THE MOON

CREATED AND WRITTEN
BY
KARLYNN KEYES
ROD BARKER

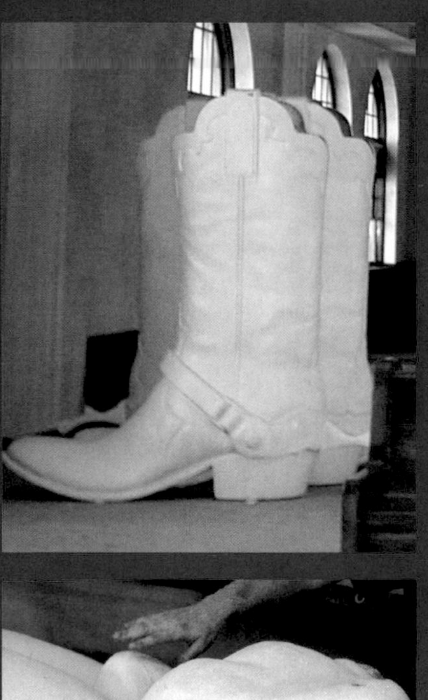

Cover Design: Bryn Wilkins, Karlynn Keyes, Fueled Media
This book was conceived by Karlynn Keyes
Written by Rod Barker
Developed by Bryn Wilkins

This book was produced by: The Trail of Painted Ponies, Inc.
and American ArtParades, LLC
P.O. Box 2629
Carefree, AZ 85377-2629
Phone: 480 459-5700 Fax: 480 361-5342
Visit our website at: www.AmericanArtParades.com

Layout and Design: Bryn Wilkins, Karlynn Keyes, Fueled Media
Design Assistants: Linda Norgren and Rikki Lodmell

ISBN-13: 978-0-9760319-3-2
ISBN-10: 0-9760319-3-0

Library of Congress Cataloging-in Publication Data available
Printed in China

FIRST EDITION

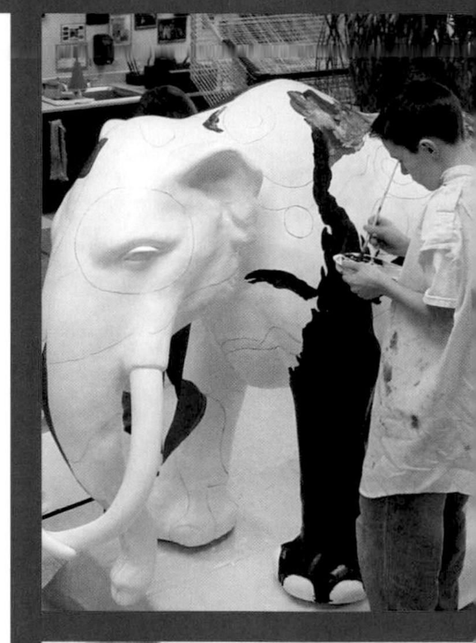

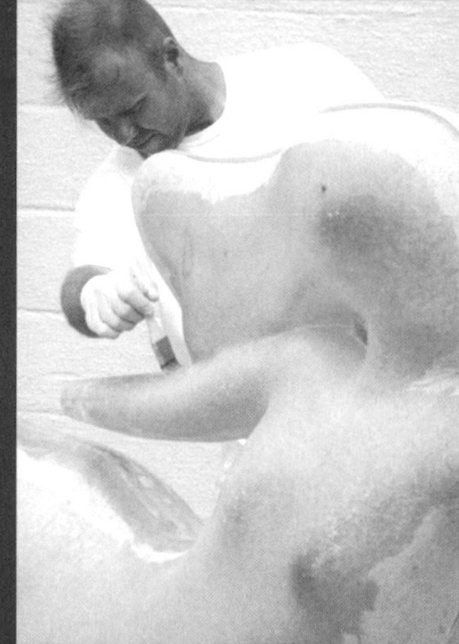

TABLE OF CONTENTS

TABLE OF CONTENTS

A*merican ArtParades* is a tribute to creativity, collaboration and compassion.

Foreword

Something extraordinary has happened to American art…it has moved out of museums and paraded right through main streets from coast to coast. Towns and cities have been transformed by bigger-than-life, fiberglass sculptures, painted by the best established and emerging artists in the country.

These inspiring outdoor exhibitions have enlivened communities and enriched the national landscape while delighting millions of people from New York to San Francisco, from Chicago to Dallas and everywhere in between. Big, bold, and uniquely American, these public art parades have sparked cultural tourism and reinvigorated the arts and downtown redevelopment, all while joyfully raising millions of dollars for worthy non-profit organizations.

By its very nature, art requires a strong sense of place and a powerful sense of purpose to thrive and *American ArtParades* captures this spirit with flying colors. American artist Grant Wood, whose talents are honored in this book with *Overalls All Over*, reminds us that you don't need to look beyond your own backyard, to find things worth celebrating. And that is exactly what these art parades are all about...creatively celebrating the cultural heritage and history of America's cities and towns through public art. These imaginative exhibitions have created an extraordinary body of original art that has captivated this entire nation.

American ArtParades introduces this sensational "New American Art Movement" to the world. This blast of creativity is truly artful entertainment that has rocked the art establishment and developed an enthusiastic audience that has turned these art parades into a new spectator sport. These exhibitions are innovative, interactive and inspiring, and they have invited people to redefine the very notion of what art is and what art can do. This is freedom of expression at its very best!

America is a culture of creativity and compassion and this is gloriously illustrated in *American ArtParades*. We invite you to take a cultural detour and explore this great country through these art parades that are filled with so much heart and soul that they have given everyone a reason to smile. Discover why we say, "Never in the history of American art have so many done so much for so many."

Karlynn Keyes
Vice President
The Trail of Painted Ponies, Inc.

Creator/Director
The Gallery at Four Seasons Resort Scottsdale

Introduction

A diverse array of provocative and innovative art experiences have made the new millennium an exciting time for those of us who believe in the importance of the arts to a vibrant society. As documented in this book, public art has assumed a leading role in this movement by taking to the streets like never before in the form of popular exhibitions themed on animal and cultural icons. "It's a zoo out there," reported one national newspaper as it reviewed the menagerie of fiberglass animal sculptures stampeding and swimming across America's urban landscapes.

The formula behind the phenomenon is simple: Select a recognizable and charismatic animal or figure that represents your community. Cultivate corporate and business sponsors to underwrite the costs of the exhibition. Invite local artists to put their creative signatures on a fiberglass form. Place the artworks strategically around the community to attract locals and visitors. Issue maps that encourage everyone to go on a sculptural treasure hunt. And then, at the end of the exhibition, auction off the festive artworks, with proceeds going to local charities and non-profit organizations.

The results have been nothing less than sensational. Disparate community elements - governments, businesses, artists, and not-for-profit organizations - have partnered on entrepreneurial joint ventures from which everyone prospers. The projects have given cities and towns a promotable identity, while increasing tourism and injecting millions of dollars into local economies. Businesses have formed creative alliances with not-for-profit organizations in a visionary paradigm for fund-raising. Taking playful delight in illustrating the unexpected possibilities of painting an unconventional canvas, artists have received career-boosting recognition.

In many ways these projects could be thought of as modern-day, artistic versions of another popular phenomenon that dates back to the latter part of the nineteenth century, when traveling circuses or parades would roll through cities and towns across America. Pulled by teams of stallions in gay plumage, sparkling floats and elaborate vehicles carrying clowns, musicians, lady performers and animal cages would parade down Main Street, set up camp for a brief stay, and, after lending color and interest and captivating the local audience, roll out of town.

To view a cow playing frisbee, a pig dancing in a sequined vest, a horse artistically souped up as a motorcycle, and to stroll among a school of fantastic fish you wouldn't find listed in any scientific journal, offers contemporary Americans a similarly joyful experience.

Of course, public art wouldn't be doing its job if it didn't generate a certain amount of controversy, and these art parades have aroused their share of detractors. Left out of the loop and unused to giving the public a say in what constitutes "art," many fine arts administrators have ridiculed the artwork because it does not include social or political commentary, but emphasizes public entertainment instead.

Overwhelmingly, however, the projects have had their champions who counter that it's time for a change of vision when it comes to the definition of "public art." It's time to "desanctify" the whole notion of art as something that has to be experienced in a museum or gallery. If handmade, graphically inventive and conceptually imaginative images aren't "art," then what are they? If the final creation doesn't meet the level of art with a capital "A" set by fine arts administrators, that is more than offset by the educational value of allowing the public to witness the artistic process at work as artists go from concept to reality, balancing color and space while completing a design. Furthermore, these projects are a great way of getting people and community groups involved in the arts, and public art in particular.

In most communities, after a run of several months, the "art parades" came to an end, leaving behind wonderful memories and a legacy of benefits. But the American art parade story does not stop there. More than offering Americans an art experience outside a traditional context, these projects introduced something thrilling to the contemporary art scene. The amazing diversity of the creative spirit they expressed, combined with their celebration in fresh aesthetic terms of what was unique about each participating city and town, succeeded in creating a new, national art community. American art parades united Americans in a unique way, and the bonding element was art.

This book captures the magic that has occurred and is still occurring on Main Street, America, while at the same time it introduces this phenomenon as an authentic American art movement. Readers are invited to take an armchair tour of the artland of America via *American ArtParades: When Pigs Flew, Guitars Rocked, and Cows Jumped Over the Moon*, and to even consider visiting these inspiring communities, where many artworks are still on display.

Rod Barker

Rod Barker
President
The Trail of Painted Ponies, Inc.

Preface

It started in Chicago in 1999 with a disarmingly simple premise: fiberglass cows decorated by mostly local artists, each commissioned and sponsored by a different business, displayed on sidewalks and in plazas and ending with a charity auction. No overarching curatorial premise, no grand theoretical construct, just simple art from and for the community at a basic level.

And what a success it was! That summer saw a community-oriented public art project on the streets of Chicago that unexpectedly generated more public interest and support than any previous temporary public art project anywhere.

Nor did it stop there. It expanded to pigs in Cincinnati and Peoria, longhorns in Plano, salmon in Seattle, people in St. Louis and Omaha, horses in Louisville, sunfish in New Orleans, Snoopys in St. Paul, ponies in New Mexico, hearts in San Francisco, labradors in Sun Valley and Racine, cod in Baltimore, bison in Salt Lake City and buffalo in Buffalo, bears, frogs, donkeys, elephants, sunflowers, American Gothic, crawfish, moose, pelicans and an almost endless list of other forms in dozens and dozens of towns and cities across America.

So where did the idea come from and how did the cows arrive in Chicago?
We must go back to the summer of 1998 when a Chicago businessman was on vacation in Zurich, Switzerland. Throughout that city, on its streets and in its public spaces, were scattered over seven hundred odd and delightful looking cows. After Peter Hanig returned home he kept thinking how much he and the other people walking around had enjoyed that unexpected display of art scattered across the urban core of a well-established city. He decided to approach the City of Chicago Department of Cultural Affairs with the idea of holding a similar project in the Windy City.

Why cows in Chicago?
The primary reason is that Zurich had done cows and Chicago was borrowing their idea. More importantly for popular perception, cows and Chicago have a long history. The myth of Mrs. O'Leary's cow and the Great Chicago Fire of 1871 as well as the Stockyards encapsulate both the destruction of the city and its economic renewal.

What happened next?
Consulting with Erna and Beat Seeberger-Quin, the Swiss artists who originated the Zurich project, Chicago decided to do a smaller version of the original project, targeting a goal of one hundred cows in the downtown area. As interest in the project grew, the scale of the project continued to expand until Chicago had more than tripled its original goal, with over three hundred cows on the streets. Sponsorships from local businesses paid the costs of the project, which replaced the more traditional single corporate underwriter model, and kept the event from being "Insert Company Name" presents the Chicago Cows. At the end of the summer about half of the cows were kept by their sponsors while the others were auctioned for charity online by Metromix and live at the Chicago Theater by Sothebys. The auctions raised nearly $3.5 million, all of which went to charities chosen by the cow's sponsor.

How to explain the success?
Artists, who were encouraged to be innovative and exercise their creativity fully, were interested in participating in a first of its kind large community-oriented public art project that was about showing their work directly to the public, not in a gallery, not in an art fair, just out there on the street. Small business people, who had not previously had the opportunity to sponsor a civic project, welcomed a fresh opportunity to support the community while promoting themselves (and they spent their marketing money on the sponsorships, directing extra hundreds of thousands of dollars directly into the pockets of Chicago's artists which would have otherwise gone into advertising expenses). The general public, visitors and residents alike, enjoyed the project as something which enriched their visit or as a summer hobby, tracking down all of the cows as they came out over the course of June, July and August.

Another fundamental reason for the cow project's success was its inherent democracy. There was no central curatorial control - artists submitted creative designs, sponsors chose the artist they wished to commission and the cow's location, while the viewing public was free to find art on the streets at any time of the day or night.

Furthermore, cows are a fairly universal and comforting animal; their cultural connections circle the world. As a large white fiberglass form they present artists with a challenging object to design and decorate but their inherent familiarity provides viewers easy access into the abstraction of art. The seriality of hundreds of repeated forms with different surface treatments in close geographic proximity creates a theme and variation experience which encourages viewers to have critical conversations and engage in aesthetic analysis of these unnatural bovines, even if that's not what the commuters and shoppers think they are talking about. Many conversations between strangers in Chicago's summer of '99 were about why one cow was better than another, why one set of color combinations was striking while a similar set was dull - that's art talk!

Why, then, did a menagerie of animals proliferate across the country?
To date, the success of the Chicago cow project has inspired close to two hundred similar projects, over eighty-five of which are featured in this book. This prodigious spread of progeny was initially due to the overwhelming popularity of the cows in Chicago. The continuing spread is now due to the proven ability of thematic object-based art projects to be done fairly simply, affordably and, if the icon chosen resonates with the community, to be tremendously popular. If the organizers have prepared well, these are usually fairly safe projects which can serve as a first step in introducing groups and communities that have not previously supported cultural projects to the benefits of supporting the arts. However, the projects are most successful when artistic quality is placed first and trust is placed in the artists to let loose their creativity and explore whatever odd juxtaposition of form and art is being sought.

Ars longa, vita brevis, moove on out.

Nathan Mason

Nathan Mason
Curator of Special Projects
Public Art Program
Department of Cultural Affairs
City of Chicago

AMERICAN
ARTPARADES

I Love A Parade!

WHEN PIGS FLEW, GUITARS ROCKED
AND COWS JUMPED OVER THE MOON
Art Rocks!
Come One, Come All.

Peanuts Around Town

Dothan, Alabama

Eye on America, Wes Hardin

Dothan's heritage is as rich as its distinguishing features are unique. Dothan prides itself on having once been home to the Alibamu and Creek Indians who were followed by timberland settlers, before townsfolk adopted the name Dothan from a biblical verse (Genesis 37:17).

Its claim to fame has been its nickname (The Peanut Capital of the World!) and its place in the Guinness Book of World Records as host to the "World's Smallest City Block" (a land triangle that features a stop sign, a yield sign and street signs).

However, something new put Dothan on the map: a dizzying array of theatrically attired, 4-foot-tall, fiberglass peanuts.

It was amazing, even startling to see how each peanut seemed to take on a personality of its very own. Their cheerful presence happily added to the impression that you can find things in Dothan that cannot be found anywhere else.

Peanuts Around Town generated new community pride and financial support for the Historic District's Festival of Murals Program, and the beautification and revitalization efforts for the Downtown Historic District.

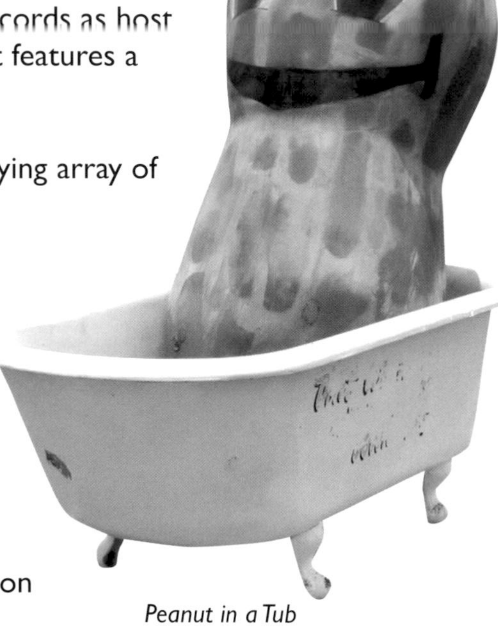

Peanut in a Tub

Firefighter
Jane G. Segrest

Nuts About Safety
Wes Hardin

Sheriff Sam
Wes Hardin

Ortho Nut
John and Melissa Rezabek

The Paper Boy
Wes Hardin

Comfort de Tours
Dave Hansen and Wes Hardin

Elvis Nut, Wes Hardin

"It was amazing, even startling to see how each peanut seemed to take on a personality of its very own."

The Peanut Producer-Star of the Wiregrass
Wes Hardin

Gone Shopping
Wes Hardin

Peanut Pride
Jane G. Segrest

Wild Salmon on Parade

Anchorage, Alaska

When the midnight sun rises in Alaska, residents and visitors know the rivers and streams will soon be teeming with wild salmon. However, the most extraordinary fish run in history took place when the wildest of wild salmon - in the form of uniquely embellished fiberglass salmon sculptures - swam up and down the city streets of Anchorage.

Since that time, these artistic wild salmon have returned faithfully each summer, remaining in their spawning grounds until the annual "Fish Fry and Buy" in September. For the price of the required fishing license (dinner tickets), anglers get to reel in their favorite catch or work of art.

To date over $120,000. has been raised to support Campfire USA, Alaska Council, The Anchorage Concert Association and the Alaska Conservation Foundation.

Copper Rvier Salmon, Virginia Armstrup

Vincent Van Coho-The Spawny Night, Jennifer Cameron

Leonardo da Fishi's The Last Supper, Debra Dubac

“On the streets of Downtown Anchorage, visitors discovered the most extraordinary fish run of all...”

Sake Salmon, Chris Floyd

South of the Border Salmon, Patricia Glatter

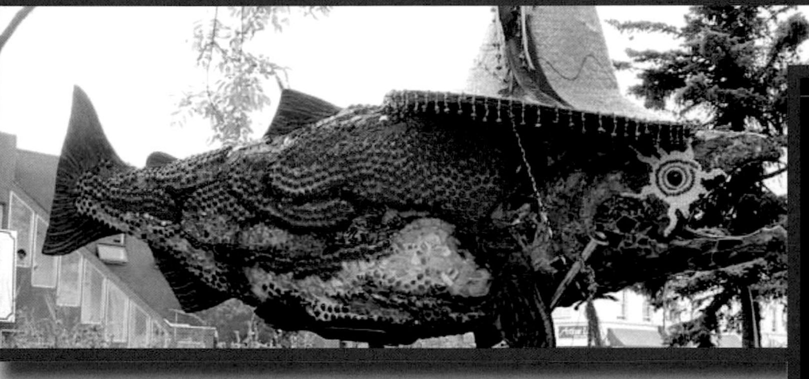

Uncle Salmon, Artisans of the Arc

Fish-O-Phone! Seventy-Six Cohos Led the Big Parade, Chris Floyd

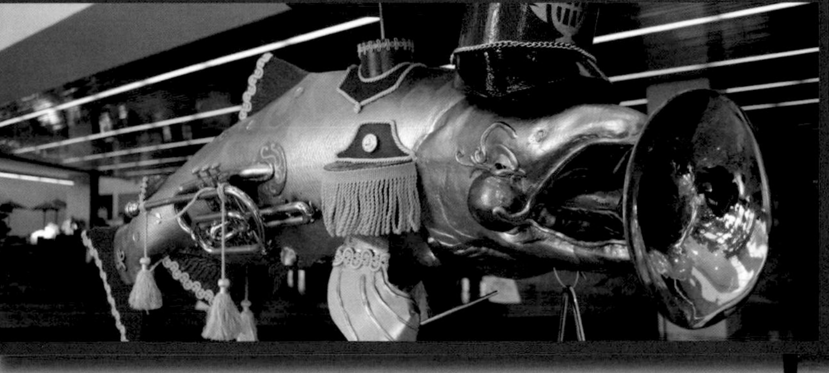

David Copper River Field, Amy and Brian Meissner

Tropical Salmon
Carol Morris Lewando, Thomas Lewando and Heather Shumar

Nascar Jack, Donald Ricker

Images above: *The Magician*, Andersen Kee, *Renewal of Life*, Natasha Isenhour, *Run for the Roses*, Janee Hughes
Image below: *Ceremonial Pony*, Cathy Smith

Born and bred in Santa Fe, New Mexico, *The Trail of Painted Ponies* was a statewide public art project that created a new paradigm, bringing communities, businesses and philanthropic organizations together in a mutually beneficial marketing partnership, with art at its center. The horse was selected because it is an American icon, and over one hundred of the best artists in the Southwest were invited to let their imaginations run wild on elegant life-size equine sculptures. Contributing their talents were such luminaries as actress Ali MacGraw, western artists JD Challenger and Amado Pena, and nationally acclaimed gourd painter Robert Rivera.

These dazzling Painted Ponies generated close to $1 million for various environmental, cultural, youth, animal and philanthropic organizations. *The Trail of Painted Ponies* was featured in an award-winning documentary film narrated by Ali MacGraw, that aired on PBS. Since that time, The Trail headquarters has moved westward to Arizona as it continues to blaze a trail into the artistic frontier.

CowPony
Lori Musil
When We Were As One
Yellowman
Route 66 Horse
Ellen Sokoloff

Reunion of the Family of Man, Cal Peacock

Anasazi Spirit Horse, Robert Rivera

As Long As There Is One, JD Challenger

"We invited artists to let their imaginations run wild...."

Karuna, Ali MacGraw

Copper Enchantment, Lynn Bean

Year of the Horse, Lori Musil

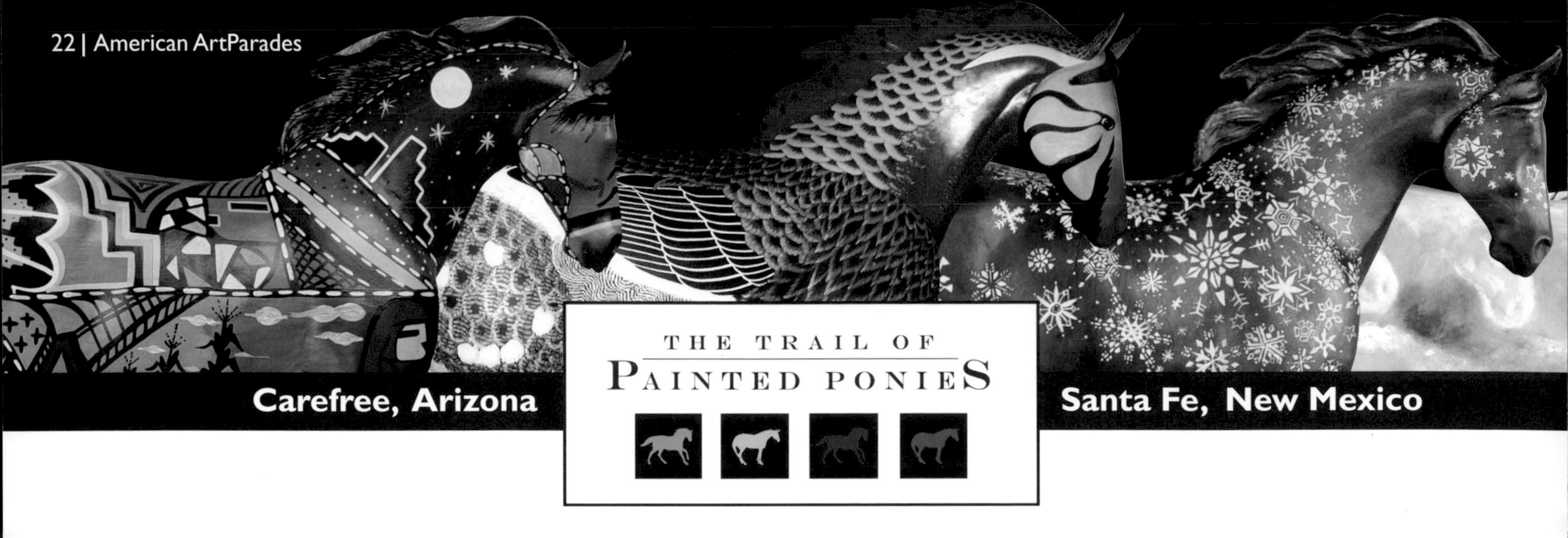

Carefree, Arizona
THE TRAIL OF
PAINTED PONIES
Santa Fe, New Mexico

The phenomenal response to the artwork generated by *The Trail of Painted Ponies* public art project prompted its organizers to continue to explore the creative possibilities of the horse as a canvas. Through a series of annual national art competitions, artists are invited to submit designs according to specified themes. The top finalists are invited to paint 2-foot tall marble-cast Masterworks and these original works of art are magnificent.

Sacred Paint
Gary Montgomery

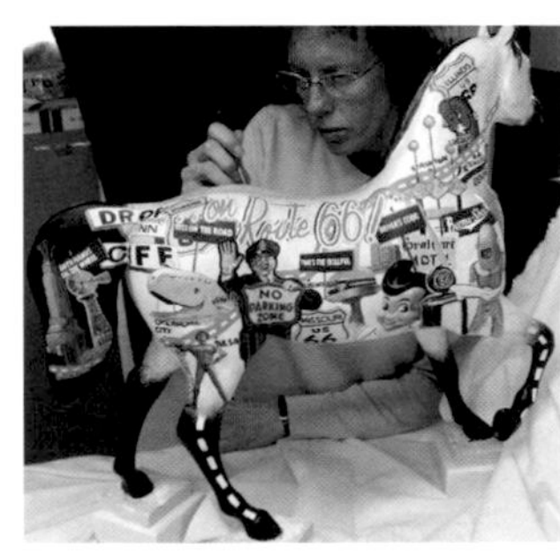

Signs of the Times
S.V. Medaris

For Spacious Skies
Janet Snyder

The first competition was titled "The Native Art of Horse Painting," and honored the Native American tradition of painting and decorating horses with dramatic colors and symbols in preparation for ceremonial events and forays into enemy territory. The second, "America the Beautiful," invited artists to conjure designs that celebrated the American West, the Spirit of America, and that unique yet quaint category of art, Americana.

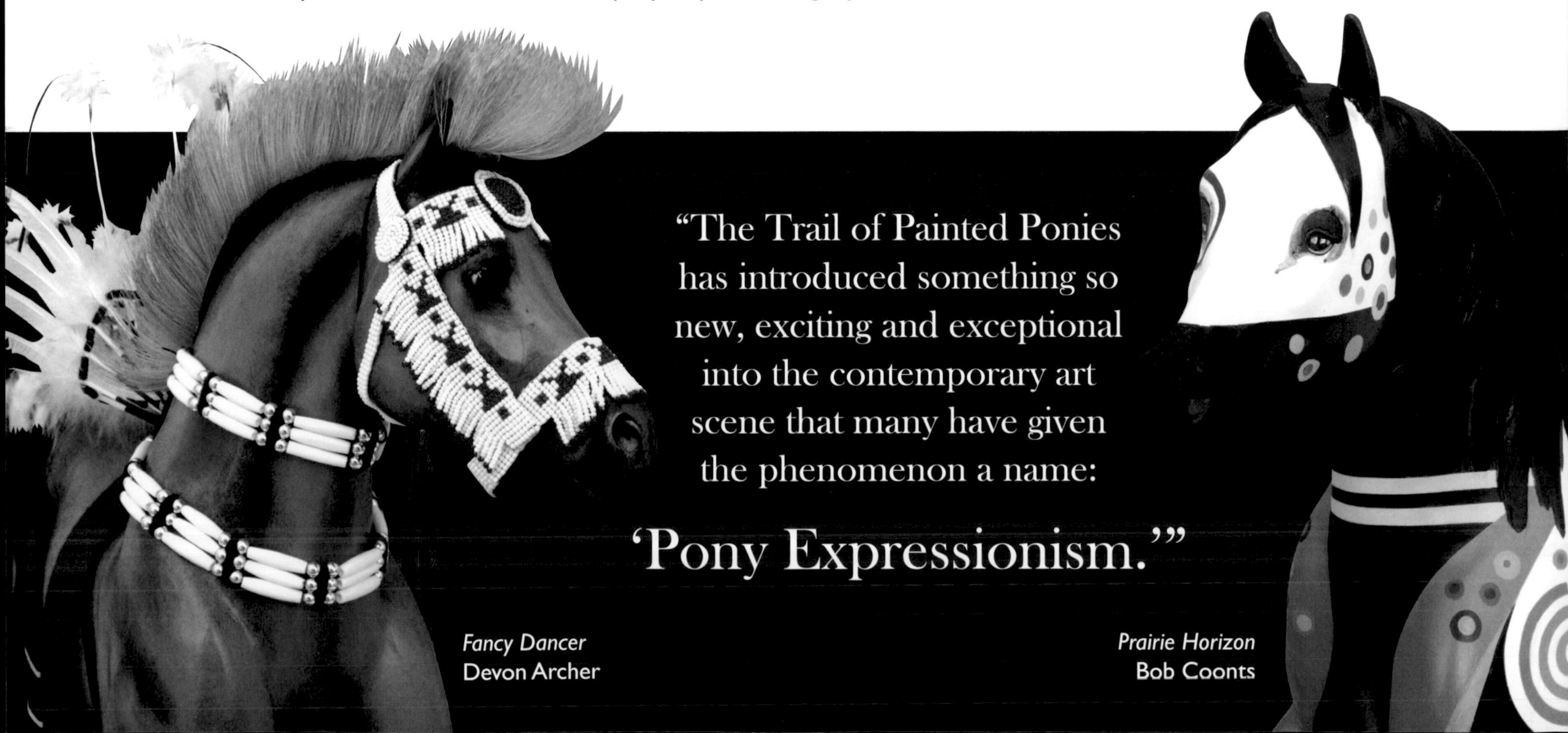

"The Trail of Painted Ponies has introduced something so new, exciting and exceptional into the contemporary art scene that many have given the phenomenon a name:

'Pony Expressionism.'"

Fancy Dancer
Devon Archer

Prairie Horizon
Bob Coonts

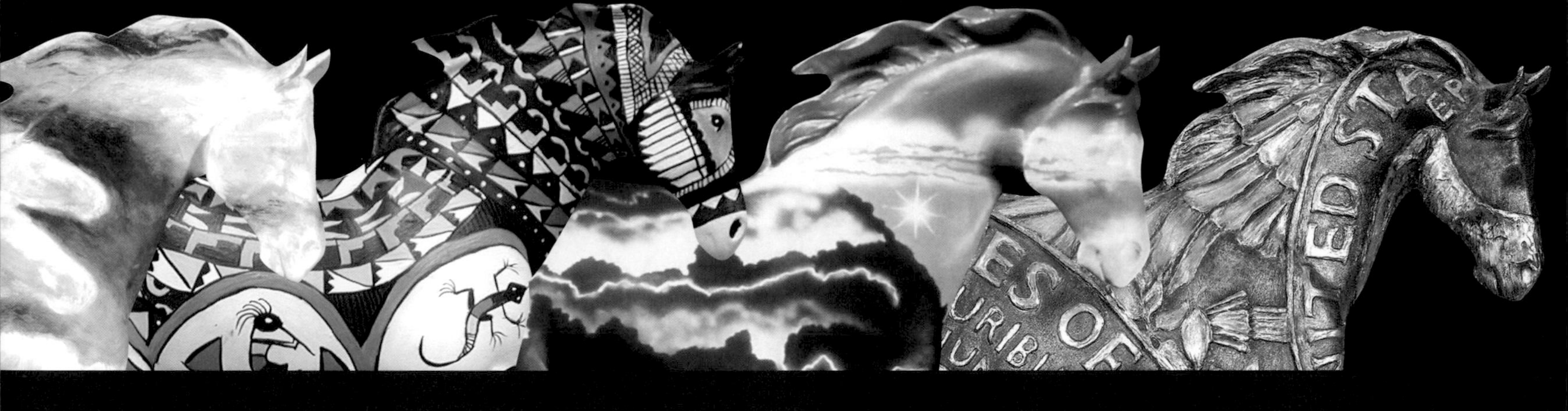

Images above left to right: *Grandfather's Journey*, Buddy Tubinaghtewa, *Horse Feathers*, Narca Moore-Craig, *Snowflake*, Judith Fudenski, *Heavenly Pony*, Noel Espinoza, *Many Tribes*, Linda Hassett, *Lightning Bolt Colt*, Dyanne Strongbow, *QuarterHorse*, Kathy Morawski

Images below left to right: *Viva Las Vegas*, La Marr, *Native Jewel Pony*, Maria Ryan, *Runs the Bitterroot*, Kevin Kilhoffer

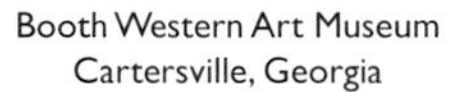

Booth Western Art Museum
Cartersville, Georgia

The Kentucky Horse Park
Lexington, Kentucky

Gallery at Four Seasons Resort
Scottsdale, Arizona

The Trail of Painted Ponies has evolved into one of the most successful fine arts and collectibles companies in the world. Original Painted Ponies continue to be exhibited at the finest museums in America, including the Booth Western Art Museum in Atlanta and the Kentucky Horse Park in Lexington, Kentucky. An extraordinary cultural partnership with the Four Seasons Resort Scottsdale has led to the creation of "The Gallery at Four Seasons Resort Scottsdale" where the entire resort is a living gallery, featuring the very best established and emerging artists in the American West. *The Trail of Painted Ponies* is committed to promoting artistic excellence and developing long-term cultural partnerships with museums, galleries, and arts organizations, nationally and internationally.

Path of the Bighorn®

Palm Springs, California

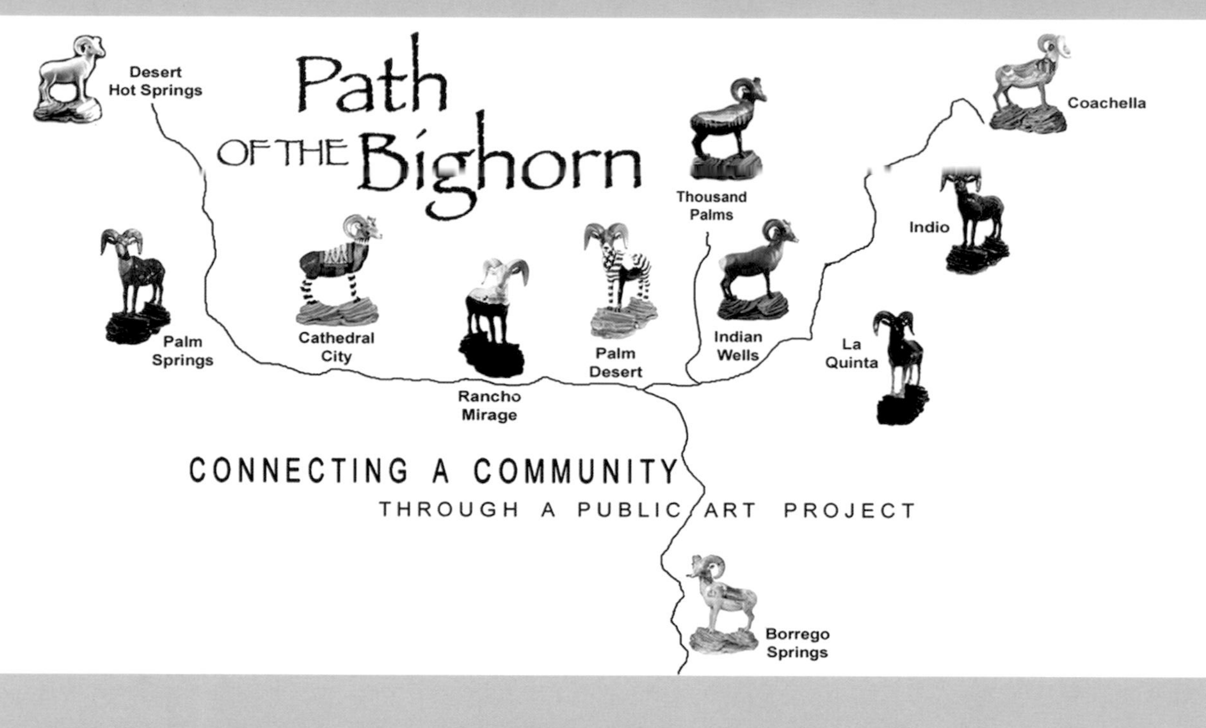

The goal was admirable: to increase awareness of the plight of the endangered Peninsular Bighorn Sheep, and to assist the Bighorn Institute with funding for research and conservation that would rescue this national treasure from the brink of extinction.

And it's not hard to imagine that there were days when, high on a barren mountaintop, silhouetted against the desert sky, these magnificent creatures paused to look down on the city of Palm Springs and wonder at the fiberglass rams below fashioned in their likeness.

International celebrities painted these sculptures with their eloquent and compelling personal visions. Some rams were covered with a brilliant array of desert flowers – just as if they had rolled in a fresh mountain pasture. Another ram wore a vision of asteroids, as if he would be viewed through 3-D glasses. There was a ram autographed by the Los Angeles Angels baseball team and a ram that glittered with thousands of Austrian crystals arranged by the singer/actress Cher.

In thanking everyone who played a part in this poignant and inspirational effort, its leading light, Alexandra Sheldon, wrote: "Thanks to their efforts, future generations will be graced by the presence of this noble creature. Because animals have no voice, we as humans are obligated to speak for them… to ensure that, for an eternity, they will be free to roam and to thrive."

Agua Caliente Young Adults and Sponsor with "Cahuilla Life"

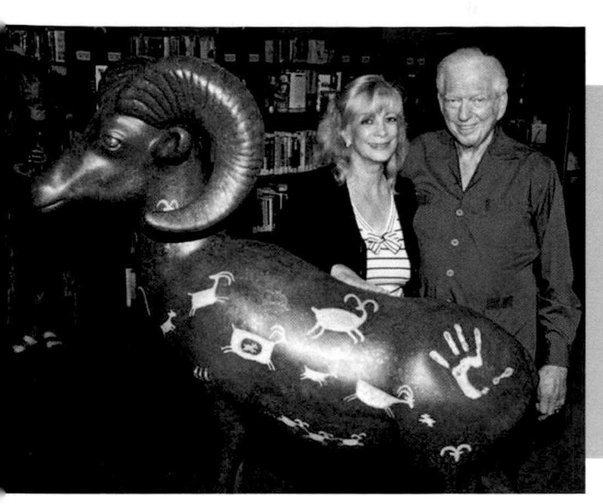

The Storyteller, Sidney and Alexandra Sheldon

Quagga, Stefanie Powers

Tequila Sunrise, Rick Farrell

Still Dreamin', Barbara Eden

"High on a barren mountaintop, silhouetted against the desert sky, these magnificent creatures paused to look down on the city and wonder at the fiberglass rams fashioned in their likeness."

Borrego, Gail Anne

Sugar, Tony Curtis

Bighorn Jack, Lori Musil

Sam the Ram, Phyllis Diller

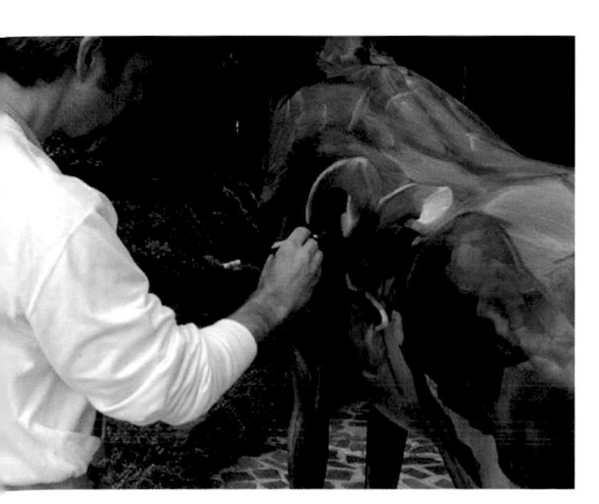

Preserve the Vision, Gregory Manchess

Aries, Bill Stout

Counting Sheep, Lisa Patencio

When the decision was made to join the national public art movement themed on an animal that had a special resonance with the city, there was very little debate in Sacramento. The mascot for the city's professional basketball team, the Sacramento Kings, was the King of the Jungle. The AAA baseball team is nicknamed the "River Cats." The primary beneficiary of the project would be the Sacramento Zoo, which enjoys a half million visitors annually and has been a part of the fabric of Sacramento for over seventy years.

The noble lion would naturally be the only animal that would be suitable for Sacramento. The next decision was what to name the project. "Pride of the Sacramento Valley" worked and was used in some circles, but the official name became *Lions on Safari*.

Sixty life-size fiberglass lions made up *Lions on Safari*, and they roamed through businesses and shopping centers around the Valley, delighting the community and visitors alike. The Sacramento Zoological Society and the Developmental Disabilities Service Organization Foundation produced *Lions on Safari*. All of the proceeds that were generated went to support these and other local non-profits.

Lions on Safari

Sacramento, California

Magic Carpet-Fly Me Away
Pat Mahoney

Mardi Growl
Judy Decker and Gretchen Ryan

Pride and Joy
Judy Arrigotti

"The Sacramento Zoo benefited when this King of the Jungle was exhibited throughout the Sacramento Valley."

Roosaline
Ted and Emma Allebes

King Tut
Michael Rosner

Arnold, King of the Capitol Lions
Hellen W. Phillips

Urban Trees

San Diego, California

San Diego prides itself on being a diverse community that has been resistant to adopting any one representational theme. So, when it came to conceiving a public art project that would: 1) showcase the world-class talent of its artists; 2) accustom the community to having large-scale sculpture within its daily environment; 3) support tourism by increasing San Diego's appeal as a cultural destination, "Urban Trees" were selected for a mile-long stretch of the most visible shoreline of San Diego Bay.

The ultimate goal was to create a pedestrian friendly environment, and to demonstrate the value of art in our everyday environment. Artists were invited to let their imaginations "sprout." The results garnered international attention. A "tree house" that consisted of colorful bird houses stacked on top of each other... a copper "trunk" with multi-colored glass leaves... aluminum seabirds that appear to take flight with the slightest breeze stood with other fabulous sculptures in planters along the waterfront pedestrian promenade of San Diego Bay. The public response was so enthusiastic that an encore exhibit was mounted.

"Artistically conceived trees would be environmentally friendly, they wouldn't need water, and like real trees, they would enhance the urban landscape."

This page, clockwise from top:
The Puzzle Tree, John S. Strokes III and Bob Archer, *Artree,* John Oleinik, *Waves of Time,* Jon Koehler

Opposite page, from top left upper row: *Symbols of San Diego, Copper Palm,* Doty and Mehner, *Arbor Urbanis Metallicus,* James Frost; Opposite page, from left middle row: *Lizardo,* Linda Joanou and Doug Snider, *Mini the Mermaid,* Frank Mando, *Forest Illuminata,* Robert G. Wertz and Julie Smith, *Surfboard Cedar Survivor,* Betsy Schulz and Hans Tegebo; Opposite page, from left bottom row: *A Different by Loving Pair,* Cecilia Stanford, *Tap Root and Growth,* Christopher Lee, *Treeway,* James A. Christopher

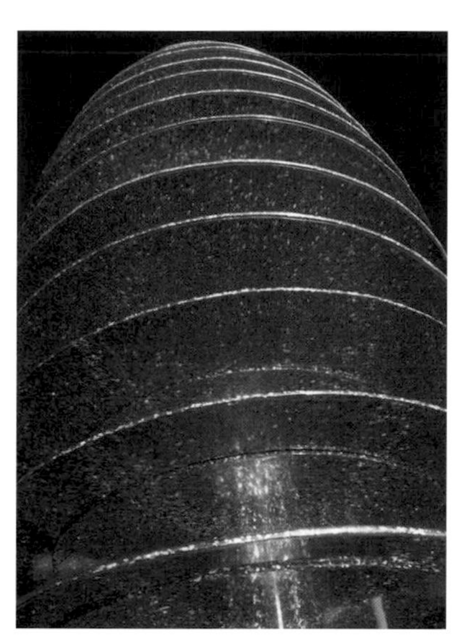

HEARTS IN SAN FRANCISCO

San Francisco, California

Unraveling Heart
Marguerite Chiang

Above from left: Coraźon de la Misi'on, Precita Eyes Muralists, *American Spirit,* Kit Hinrichs, *My Brother, My Heart,* Marianne Fay

The Heart was chosen to reflect a city that is recognized for its acceptance and tolerance, as well as being perennially "open-hearted."

Hearts in San Francisco debuted in Union Square on Valentine's Day, with two hearts and high hopes: to stage a citywide outdoor "heart exhibit" and to raise over $2 million for the San Francisco General Hospital Foundation. As the spring turned to summer, hearts appeared everywhere, from the Marina to Yerba Buena, from the foggy end of town to the edge of the Bay. Legendary musician and Heart artist Tony Bennett created a heart for permanent display in Union Square as a gift to the people of San Francisco.

The sculptures were as diverse as the artists who created them, and as all of those who call San Francisco home. There were red hearts and gold hearts and hearts of many colors. There was a heart that glowed white, and a heart that was black. There were hearts featuring romance and hearts that depicted loss. Nitty-gritty hearts, highly polished hearts and quiet, contemplative hearts.

The sculptures also held memories and inspiration, poetry and mystery. Behind the "public heart" were the artists' personal stories. Together, the art and the anecdotes were a true testimonial to creativity and resilience, to the wonderful ways in which we are different, and the fundamental ways in which "all hearts beat the same."

USPS Love Stamp, Michael Osborne

"Legendary musican and Heart artist
Tony Bennett
created a Heart
for permanent display in Union Square
as a gift to the people of
San Francisco."

Entangled Heart, Tor Archer

Beat-Heart-Beat, David Povilaitis

The Tempest Cozy, Adele Louise Shaw

Heartsy Poppies, Gary Bukovnik

San Jose, California

Sharks were a logical icon for San Jose, given its proximity to the Pacific Ocean and the name of its professional hockey team. Through painting, welding, sculpting or adding mechanical features, one hundred of these feared, finned fiends-of-the-deep were transformed into whimsical, quirky, amusing and interesting works of interactive art that circled the downtown area. Shark encounters happened while walking down the street, playing in a local park, and even in unsuspecting office lobbies. Colorful schools of sharks swam alongside downtown's urban landmarks.

Even soon-to-be Governor Arnold Schwarzenegger was bitten by shark fever when he created his idea of finned fine art titled "Shark and Stripes."

From ballerinas to butterflies…from leopards to light towers…from sushi to submarines…*SharkByte Art*™ added a definitive twist to artistic expression in San Jose. And, when the time came to bid on a shark, a list of reasons to buy were playfully provided:

1) Use it as a passenger in your auto for the carpool lane (just kidding).
2) Hang it over the mantle of your fireplace and tell your friends you caught it off Cabo San Lucas.
3) Display it in the backyard. They make great garden decorations and scarecrows.
4) Take it to a movie (you'll get good seats, trust us).

Collectors began to circle at the site of the auction and soon a feeding frenzy began. When it was over, hundreds of thousands of dollars had been raised to benefit more than eighty non-profit organizations in San Jose.

Carmen Sharkana, Denise Satter

The Little Ballerina Shark
Chuck E. Foltz

Frankenshark
David Choe for Kids at Teach For America San Jose

deFINitely Downtown
Sonya Paz

Shark & Stripes
Rohit Sabharwal and Arnold Schwarzenegger

"One hundred of these feared, finned fiends-of-the-deep were transformed into whimsical, quirky, amusing and interesting works of art."

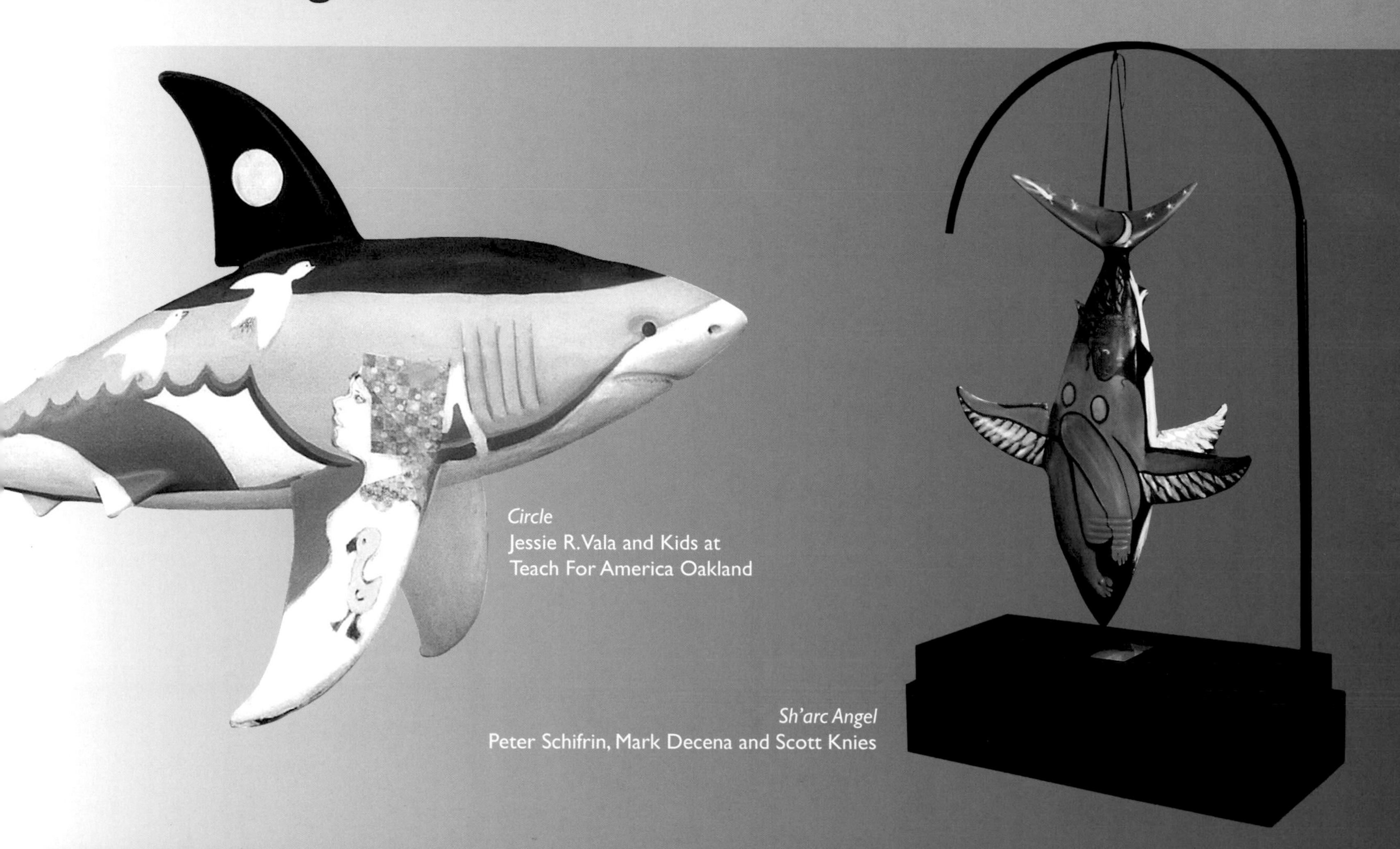

Circle
Jessie R. Vala and Kids at Teach For America Oakland

Sh'arc Angel
Peter Schifrin, Mark Decena and Scott Knies

Trout About Downtown

San Luis Obispo, California

This page, top to bottom:
What Wine Goes With Trout? Sandra Kay Johnson,
Trout On The Range, Lori Krivacsy,
Steelina La Queena, Sue Palmer,
Fish Doctors, Mathias Work,
Water Taxi, Josephine Crawford

San Luis Obispo is a beautiful seaside city and one of California's oldest communities, having begun with the founding of Mission San Luis Obispo de Tolosa in 1772. With *Trout About Downtown* it distinguished itself another way, this time with an artistic tribute to Steelhead Trout.

Organized by the "Fish Commish," a moniker used to describe a collaboration among several community groups such as Friends of Prado Day Center, the Chamber of Commerce, the Downtown Association, and the local arts community, the painted Trout, standing 5-foot tall, were strategically placed around the downtown area in a way that allowed them to be viewed by a self-guided tour in one hour. After gracing San Luis Obispo for several months, they were reeled in and auctioned off, the proceeds from this "catch" benefiting the Prado Day Center, which serves needy children and families.

"It's an odd thing to choose a fish.
But it is a fun shape. You can do a lot with it."

This Page, clockwise from top:
Gogh Trout Gogh
Laguna Middle School's Art Class,
William Randolph Trout
Otto Schmidt,
Artie - Angling For Assets
Jack Foster,
Return of the Trout
Annie Bauman,
The Heart of SLO
Eve Ann,
Steely Dan
Jake Ballweber,
Hot Rod Trout
Jim Valentine

Ban Bare Bears

Colorado Springs, Colorado

Images above from left to right: *Dancing In The Moonlight*, Deb Komitor, *Ursa Major*, Sara Ware Howsam, *Summer In The Suburbs*, Deb Komitor, *Hot Rod Bear*, Tom Heaney, *Navajo Bear*, Jennifer Bush, *Colorado Landscape*, Felta Hall, *Natasha Bear*, Carolyn Intemann, *Belli The Bear*, Anthony Meneses of Workout Ltd.

"A variety of artists transformed dozens of fiberglass bears into beary well-dressed statues."

Dressed for success took on new meaning for the Colorado Springs business community when a variety of artists transformed dozens of fiberglass bears into "beary" well-dressed statues. A law firm designed a bear wearing traditional barrister garb and named it "Bearrister Bear." The classic scene in the movie "Gentlemen Prefer Blondes" where Marilyn Monroe is trying to keep her skirt down inspired "Bearilyn Monroe." This Colorado public art project brought artists and the community together to raise awareness and funds for the Pikes Peak Foundation for Mental Health.

Durango, Colorado

"Pumas on Parade embraced the concept of public art for public land."

Oaxacan Dreaming, Mike McPherson

The San Juan Mountains Association *Pumas on Parade* campaign was created around the amazing mountain lion – a compelling symbol of the power of nature and a species that is integral to a healthy ecosystem. The puma, a cautious and cagey Four Corners' native, is arguably the most majestic animal on the region's public lands. This elusive predator also epitomizes the intense conflicts triggered by human-wildlife proximity.

With *Pumas on Parade*, SJMA embraced the concept of public art for public land. The project effectively used public art as a platform to engage local talent, teach resource and wildlife values, and to support the organization's programs to care for irreplaceable public lands. Each Puma design reflected the individual creator's inspiration, drawn from personal history and experience on the landscape. Most importantly, nearly all of the Pumas remain on permanent public display – allowing visitors to Durango to continue to bask in their beauty and learn from their legacy.

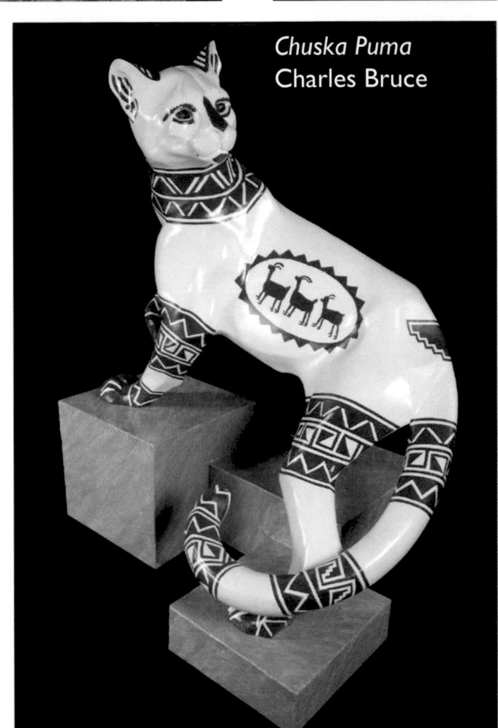

Chuska Puma
Charles Bruce

Leave Only Footprints
Bonnie Bryant

Radiant Cat
Claudia DeLong

San Puma de Las Animas y Plata
Shan and Regina Wells

Cascading Camouflage
Eileen Fjerstad

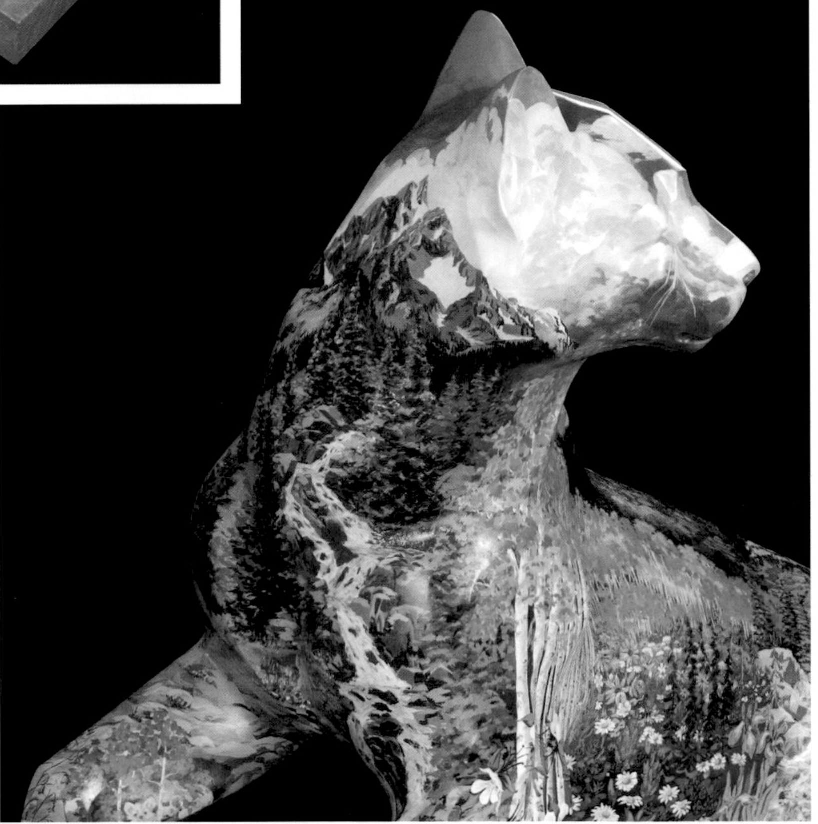

GEESE GALORE

Longmont, Colorado

Canadian Geese are a familiar part of the Longmont, Colorado landscape. They swim in the lakes, nest in the fields, crisscross the skies in flight. There's a saying in these parts:

"Longmont wouldn't be Longmont without its geese."

But there was something very different about the geese in *Geese Galore*. They stood 7-feet tall and sported fantastic plumage that you wouldn't find in any field guide. They flocked in neighborhoods, city parks and downtown Longmont. With names like "Little Deuce Goose", "Fowl Play" and "I Love Lucy Goosey", they turned heads and stopped traffic. They even hatched a display of smaller decoys in store windows and front yards around town. Visitors to town were encouraged to go on a wild goose chase….

And when the time came for the real geese to fly south, the artistic geese were auctioned at the Longmont Museum, raising money and awareness for arts and cultural organizations, and advancing Longmont's reputation as an arts destination.

Glamorous Goose
Becky and Chuck Everitt

Sister Cities Goose
Lory Ohs and Beau Townsend

Still Life with Goose
Linda Juhl and Stephanie Hilvitz

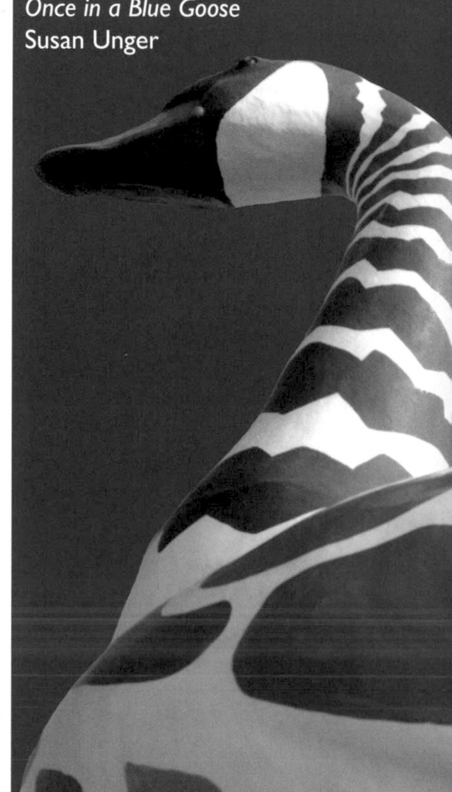

Once in a Blue Goose
Susan Unger

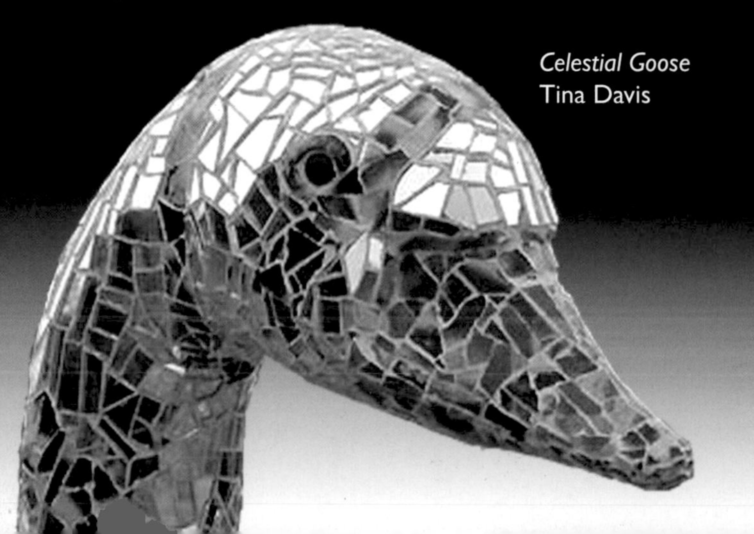

Celestial Goose
Tina Davis

Tulips LaGoose
Carol Balliet

Benjamin Franklin Goose
Darlene Valentine

Tropical Goose
Danny Pickett

Nestling Mother Goose
Marie Gibbons

Moo Goose
Tori Gardner

I Love Lucy Goosey
Dawn Hessel, Sandy Jensen
and Adrienne Yauk

The Ironclad Robo-Goosinator
Will Brown

GALAXY of STARS

Follow Your Star
Miggs Burroughs

Darien
New Canaan
Norwalk
Wilton
Weston
Westport
CONNECTICUT

It was a natural convergence. STAR Inc. is a not-for-profit agency serving people with developmental disabilities in a cluster of Connecticut communities. Their 50th anniversary was coming up and thought was being given as to how to celebrate this significant date in a way that raised awareness and money for the organization. Across the country, amusingly surreal fiberglass sculptures were popping up on city streets, entertaining everyone before they were sold to benefit charities.

And in this way, a *Galaxy of Stars* was born. Fifty, 5-foot by 5-foot gloriously painted stars, one for each year of STAR's existence, were sprinkled throughout Connecticut communities. The sky was the limit, with *Galaxy of Stars* lighting the way.

Adding star power to the event was a star autographed by President George W. Bush, while another sported the signatures of all of the New York Mets baseball players. It was an occasion when even the politicians put aside their differences, as Connecticut Senator Christopher Dodd, a Democrat, and Congressman Christopher Shays, a Republican, joined together in this "celebration of the human spirit." While STAR Inc. was the "official" beneficiary of this sparkling public art project, the true beneficiaries were the people it serves.

Blooming Star, Kathleen Lee

Stars of Our Community, Martha Perske

STARfish Aquarium, Zoe Dyson Hedstrom

STAR Cycle, Janet Luongo

Filmstar, Leona Frank

STAR of the Free, Alexander Garnett

"The sky was the limit with a *Galaxy of Stars* lighting the way."

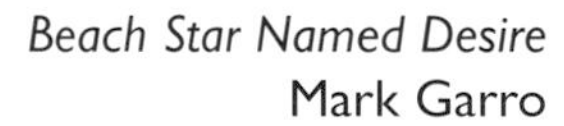

Beach Star Named Desire
Mark Garro

Seastar, Anne Jayson

Sun, Moon & Stars, Jan Raymond

Your Fate Is in the STARs
Gordon Micunis

TransiSTAR, Phillip Dolcetti

DINO DAYS

Wilmington, Delaware

What's worth doing once, when it's successful, is worth doing a second and third time! That was the theory behind a series of public art projects designed to revitalize the once-booming downtown of Wilmington, Delaware.

Dino Days represented all aspects of Wilmington, from its history to its endless fascination with NASCAR®. The Delaware College of Art and Design benefited from the proceeds of this public art project.

Due to the Dino's overwhelming popularity, another herd was hatched the following year, which proved to be just as successful. This led to yet another public art project, *Cool City Cars,* which had an exciting twist: artists were invited to get behind the artistic wheel of a "cool car" and rev up their imaginations, which is exactly what the Christina Cultural Arts Center was hoping for, since they were the benificiary.

The city of Wilmington continued their commitment to public art with the creation of *Wilmington Wonderland*, which featured creatively decorated snowmen that warmed the hearts of residents and visitors alike before they melted away, leaving a legacy of good will and financial support for the United Way of Delaware and the Christina Cultural Arts Center. The Wilmington Renaissance Corporation in partnership with DuPont and the Office of the Mayor developed all of Wilmington's Public Art Projects.

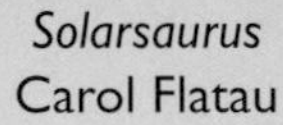

Solarsaurus
Carol Flatau

DuPontosaurus
Sam Bass

Holly del Dino
Cynthia McGrellis

Tinkerbellasaurus
Erica Hatch

Four Scoreasaurus
Matt Cummiskey

Clockwise from above left:
Ace Crashed-a-don, Dorian and Lizz Angello
Urban Chameleon, Annabel Ferguson
Spider Delrex, Christy Tapert with the Dover Art League
Slinky-Saurus, Rich Hanel and Toniann DeGregory
with Cab Calloway School of the Arts
Dinersaurus, AB & C Creative Team
Mr. T Rex, Guy F. Tenaro

COOL CITY *cars*

Wilmington, Delaware

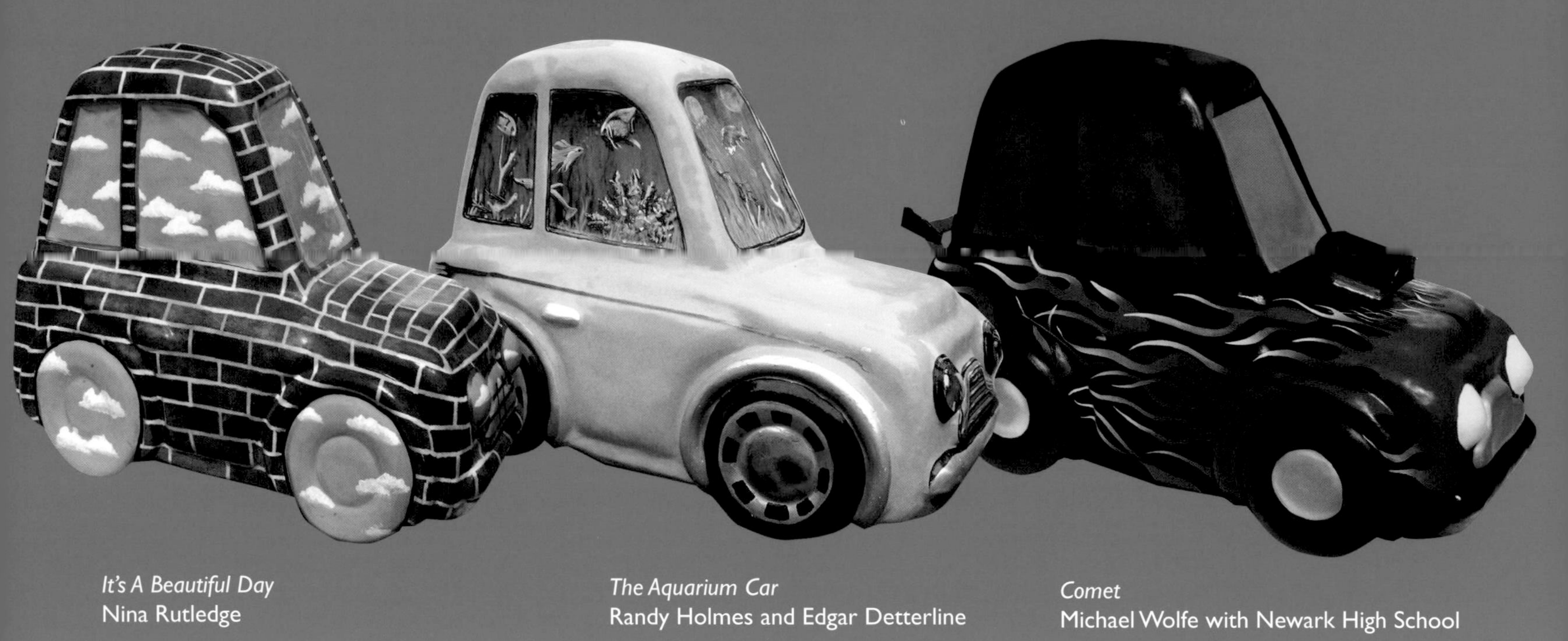

It's A Beautiful Day
Nina Rutledge

The Aquarium Car
Randy Holmes and Edgar Detterline

Comet
Michael Wolfe with Newark High School

"Artists were invited to get behind the artistic wheel of a 'cool car' and rev up their imaginations."

The Secrets of the Deep
Greg Shelton

Wilmington's Finest
Guy F. Tenaro and Laura Gonce

Flower Power
Erica Hatch

Ladybug Lady
Donna L. Downs

Produce Pick-Up
Samantha Raftovich,
Angelina and Blaise Saienni

Nemobile
Christy Tapert and Nick Wasileski

Revolution
Nick Wasileski and Christy Tapert

Car-penter
Susan B. Reed

Wilmington Wonderland

Wilmington, Delaware

Images above left to right: *Bee Yourself*, David Ciommo, *Jazzy Brown*, Vicki Rinalda McGill, *Mr. Snow-it-all*, Justin Jackson-Cherry, *Ice Chef*, William and Barbara Gordon, *Conehead*, Margaret Finch, *Snow Way, Jose'*, Susan B. Reed, *Uncle Pennybags*, Donna Downs and Christine Paoli with St. Edmond's Academy, *Swirly*, William and Barbara Gordon

"With clever names like 'Snow way Jose' and 'Mr. Snow-It-All,' the whimsical snowmen warmed hearts..."

King Snowmankahmen
Laurette Kovary and Leslie Dixon

Captain Cold
David R. Ziegler III and David Ziegler IV

Off Course
Thomas and Rose Ann Truselo

Timeless
Zora Janosova

Party Animals

Washington, DC

In a city notorious for taking itself too seriously, *Party Animals* provided an opportunity to have some fun, in addition to exhibiting the extraordinary artistic talent thriving in and around the nation's capital.

Party Animals was launched by First Lady Laura Bush who provided the background to the mascots for the Republican and Democratic Party that served as the two forms for *Party Animals*: "The donkey and the elephant first appeared in public in the 1870s - in *Harper's Weekly* magazine, when political cartoonist Thomas Nast used them to make satirical jabs at the politicians of the day. You might say that his efforts backfired: the animals have instead become much-loved symbols of American politics."

And so it was only natural that visitors to Washington, DC were encouraged to take a "Party Animal Safari" and roam the District to discover the two hundred whimsical donkeys and elephants that had stampeded throughout the Nation's Capital. *Party Animals* attracted international media and rave reviews, all while raising over $1.2 million for artist grants and arts education programs through the DC Commission on the Arts and Humanities.

America the Beautiful
Di Stovall

"Donkeys and elephants have become much-loved symbols of American politics."

Periodic Table of the Elephants
Patapsco High School

Just Visiting
Mary Fran Miklitsch

Citiphant
Anne Marchand

After Peaceable Kingdom
Lisa Farrell

Watermellophant
Lola Lombard

Brownstone, Marble, and Trees
Jody Berstesser

Lucky Don Keystador
Melissa Shatto

Strom
Thomas Farrell, Chad Allen, and their friends

Barn Raising
Ellen Sinel

Panoramic Pachyderm
Jody Wright

Pandamania

Washington, DC

"Even Confucius would be speechless at the sight of Pandamania."

Poppy Panda, Roberta Marovelli

Year of the Panda, Nicholas Shi

So talked-about were the *Party Animals* that the DC Commission on the Arts and Humanities decided to follow up with a second citywide public art project that featured yet another new species of public art... the Giant Panda!

The selection of the adorable panda was a natural, given the phenomenal popularity of these cuddly creatures since their arrival at the National Zoo in 1972. *Pandamania* featured over one hundred fifty artistically designed large-scale panda sculptures that were just like the Giant Pandas themselves: charming, engaging, and adorable. Proceeds from the Giant Panda Auction supported the Arts Commission's activities and programs.

Threatened Species
Rufus Toomey

China Doll
Amy Goodstine and Brandon Bloch

Pandy Warhol
Margaret Finch

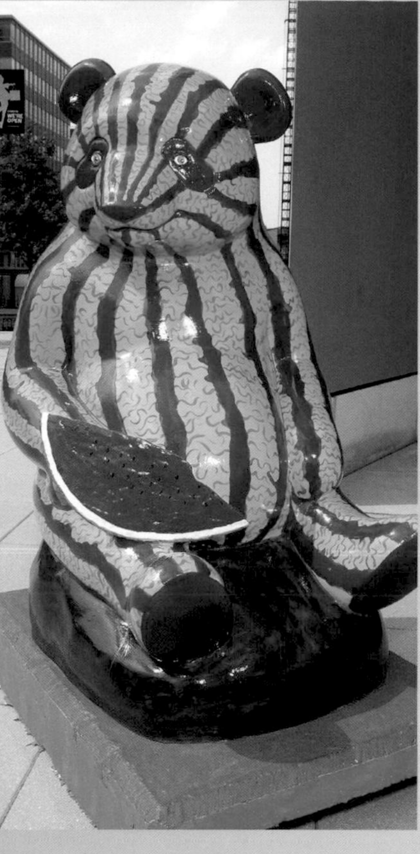

Panda Melon
Anthea Zeltzman

DC's Choo-Choo
Claude Andaloro

Perennial Panda
John Bledsoe

Pandela Anderson
Maggie O'Neill

Panda Van Gogh
Kevin Richardson

Chocolate Dipped Strawbeary
Debbie Smith Mezzetta

Papillion Bear
Robert Dixon-Gumm

Dolphins on Parade™

Key West, Florida

What's the Porpoise of Stars & Angels?
Jeannine Bean

Carmina Marina Dollfina
Leslie Kanter

Bottlenose Beach
John David Hawver

Images left, top to bottom: *Charlie the Dolphin,* Barbara Bowers, *Bougie the Bloomin Dolphin,* Bouganvillea House Artists, *Cyber Fish,* Greg Scorzafave, *Tennessee Williams,* Karen Laake

Imagine what the first Spanish explorers, approaching the Florida shores in the 16th Century, would have thought if, welcoming them up and down the necklace of islands now known as the Florida Keys, had been *Dolphins on Parade*™ - one hundred wildly embellished, dolphin sculptures.

Locals and tourists were treated to just such a fantastic site when this 100-mile long, aquatic celebration of whimsy, stretching from Key Largo to Key West, added a colorful chapter to the romantic history of South Florida. As the sun set on *Dolphins on Parade*™, grants were awarded to local artists to encourage them to keep creativity flowing in the Keys.

"A 100-mile long, aquatic celebration of whimsy, stretching from Key Largo to Key West."

Miss American Pie
Captain Outrageous

Don Shoe Less
Monte Triz

He-She
Kate Peachey

Images below, left to right: *Woody,* Jonathan Shonting, *Marbles,* Mel Fisher Kids, *Piggy Back Dive,* Barbara Grob, *The Day the Sun Didn't Set,* Judi Brandord, *Dolphin Dreams,* Olga Manosalvas

We Let The Dawgs Out

Athens, Georgia

Carmen Mirandawg, Cathe and Ron Stein

The bulldog named "UGA" is the University of Georgia's mascot, and is said to be the most beloved college mascot in the world! He has been featured in books, starred in movies, and even appeared on the cover of *Sports Illustrated*. What more natural icon for Athens to choose than the "Bulldawgs!"

Although many communities auctioned their works of art to raise money for charities, *We Let The Dawgs Out* chose to leave the Bulldawgs on display, transforming their city into an outdoor museum. Inevitably, when a story about Athens was written, one of the "Bulldawgs" was featured, which explains how "Caesar Dawgustus" appeared on the front of the travel section of the *L.A. Times*.

Opposite page from top, left to right: *Sunflower,* Robin Fay, *Ol' Silver,* Kelly Stevens, *Dawg Walker,* Chris Wyrick, *Three B's Canine - Georgia Red Clay Dawg,* Cameron Zareie, *Reflection of a Classic City,* Charlotte House, *Dawgwood Bark,* James Carroll

"What more natural icon for Athens

Bugga, Bruce MacPherson

Vincent Van Go Dawg, Kathy Whitehead

to choose than the Bulldawgs?"

Ceasar Dawgustus, Gretchen Fennell

Thurston LaDonnahue III, Scott Sosebee

Sky Dawg, Kathy Whitehead

Tybee Turtle Tour

Tybee Island, Georgia

Ma Cootah enn Lee' Ones, Don Josephson

The *Tybee Turtle Tour* was designed as a public art experience that connected the unique barrier island turtle nesting environment with a colorful and diverse art colony. Tybee Island depends on visitors to keep its economy viable, and so the Tybee Arts Association chose a fun island-inclusive event that had a humorous side but delivered an important message: YOU CAN HELP SAVE TURTLES!

Education about endangered sea turtles and barrier island ecology was woven into this facinating tour of oversized fiberglass turtle sculptures that were placed all over the island. Visitors were educated to the plight of the turtles and fifty percent of the *Tybee Turtle Tour* profits went to support the Tybee Marine Science Center and The Tybee Arts Association.

Images below, Top: Myrtle Turtle
Bottom: Bert Turtle

Tybee Tourist Turtles - Bert & Myrtle, Myke Knutsen and Joy Flynn

Turtle Vision, Sally Bostwick

Mermaid Rodeo Bareback Rider
Samantha Claar

"YOU CAN HELP SAVE TURTLES!"

Ma Cootah enn Lee' Ones, Don Josephson

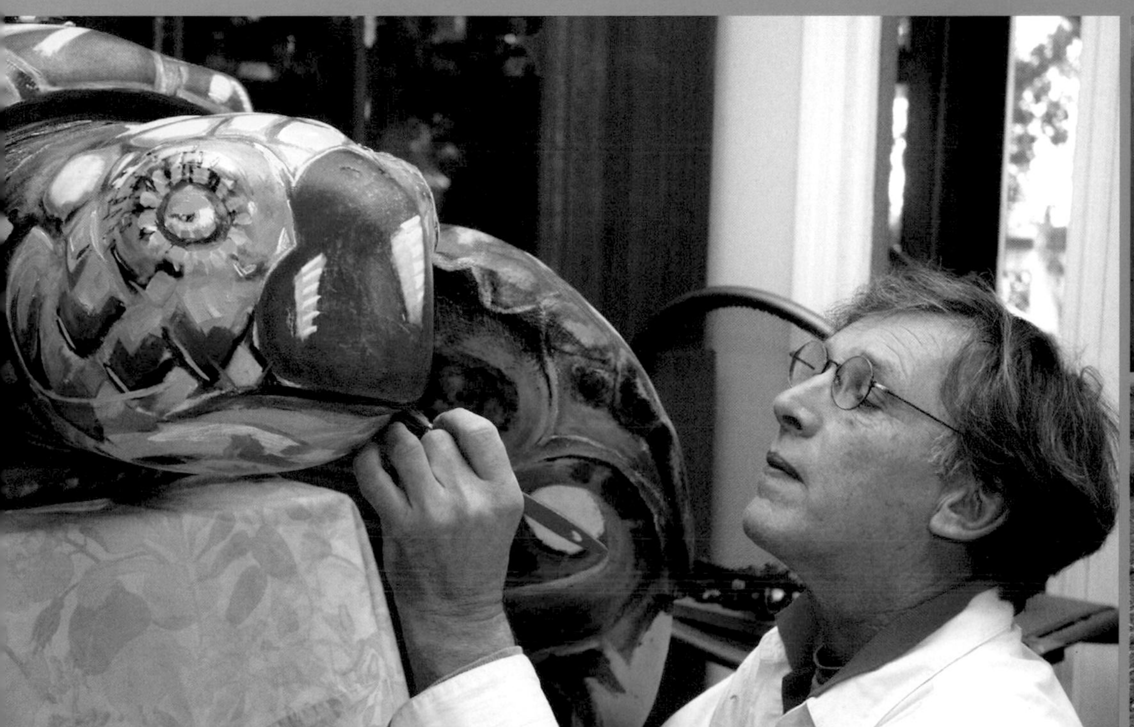

Images below top: *Hey Diddle Turtle*, Deborah Mosch
Bottom: *Shellter*, Dale Clifford

Mirrored Gecko
Paul K. Guncheon

Many people might ask, "Why a 5-foot gecko?" The answer is: What better icon of Hawaii's character is there than the gecko (Mo'o in Hawaiian). Most islanders and visitors have heard the chirps of this tiny little lizard calling and look to find a little one perched on a broad leaf or rafter, eyeing them suspiciously. The gecko figure, by master artist Rochelle Lum, in itself offers great depth of personality, and as a blank canvas it provided a unique form for the talents of local artists.

Picture this: a lounging sunbathing gecko, complete with sunglasses and an umbrella drink; a surfing gecko leashed to a board; a Pollock-inspired "Jackson P. Gecko" … all slithering on the streets of Waikiki and downtown Honolulu. These truly were *Geckos in Paradise*.

"I don't make art as much as I make magic," said one of the artists. He was speaking for himself, but he could just as easily have been speaking for everyone who turned a gecko into a work of art.

*Geckos in Paradise*SM transformed the landscape of Honolulu when fifty sculpted fiberglass geckos decended upon the island city. This fantastic arts event raised awareness of women's health with all of the proceeds supporting the Breast Center at Kapi'olani Medical Center. The entire event was organized by the Kapi'olani Health Foundation.

Rainbow Gecko
The Hawaii Potter's Guild

Royal Hawaiian Flyin' Gecko
Linda Kane

 # Gecko 1:65000
Conan Smith

And all that Jazz
Maritz

Ki `i Kapa Mo`o
Lynn Cook

Sid
Jinja Kim

The Auana Gecko
Anthony Randall

Camouflage Gecko Hawaiian Style
Patrice A. Federspiel

"I don't make art as much as I make magic."

Art Gecko
Kitty Cantrell

Sunburned Gecko
Claudia Wallace

Astro Gecko
Margo Goodwill

Mo`o`ili `ili
Grant Kagimoto

Dragon Gecko
Behlke and Moriaz

The Sunbather
Doug Young

The Red-Winged, Gold-Crested Gecko
Bernice Akamine

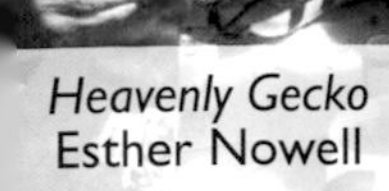

Heavenly Gecko
Esther Nowell

Future Gecko Technology
Sam Clemens

Pineapple Gecko
Jeff Langcoan

The Conductor
Judy Kawabata

Rainbow Gecko
Shawn Ardonin

Geckoman
Ingrid Manzione

Coeur d'Alene, Idaho

Coeur d'Moose
Maria Ryan

Monarch Moose
Michael Horswill

Inspired by the Federal Educational Program "No Child Left Behind," which is designed to improve the nation's public schools, Coeur d'Alene decided to merge art with its schools and community in a captivating tribute to a creature that is integral to the northwest environment. And so, *No Moose Left Behind* lumbered into town.

So spectacular were the results that its mayor declared, "When I see each and every moose, I am delighted by the absurdity of seeing a multicolored, wild animal in the middle of a sidewalk or on a grass lawn. Their magical nature reminds me of the pleasure children find in their first finger-painting project, their first picture book, and their first favorite teacher. These moose inspire the creative spark in all of us, and at its best, education does just that."

From playful and vibrant designs that reflected the majestic, mysterious, goofy nature of the moose, to impressionistic depictions of the lush woods, lakes and rivers in the surrounding area, to whimsical homages to vintage cartoons such as "Rocky & Bullwinkle," no moose was left behind.

The EXCEL Foundation, Inc. also made sure that no teachers were left behind by creating an Endowment Fund to provide teachers in the Coeur d'Alene School District with grant awards that have so far totaled close to $500,000.

Tribal Tatoose
Denise Bartlett

Moose Tracks: Gathering the Strays
Yvonne Benzinger

Anatomy of Timeber; What Moose?
Ken Spiering

First Man on the Moose
Jennifer Riggs

Precious Metals Moose
Laurie Schafer

KRONOS the Time Traveler
Janine Wood-Bokman

Moose Along Cassidy-Nature Guide
Kay O'Rourke

Dancing in the Belly of Idaho
Mary Dee Dodge

Matilda
Stephen Strickland

"Their magical nature reminds me of the pleasure children find in their first finger-painting project, their first picture book, and their first favorite teacher."

Little Deuce Moose
David Clemons

Bloomin' Moose
Georgianna Hylton

Digging Water Patatoes Along Lake Coeur d'Alene, George Flett

Sacred Walk
J. Nelson

Rockin' Raffle Moose
Jan Wilhelmi

Walk Softly and Look for Tracks
Greg Torline

Salmon Mousse
Melissa Cole

Espresso To Go
Virginia Carter

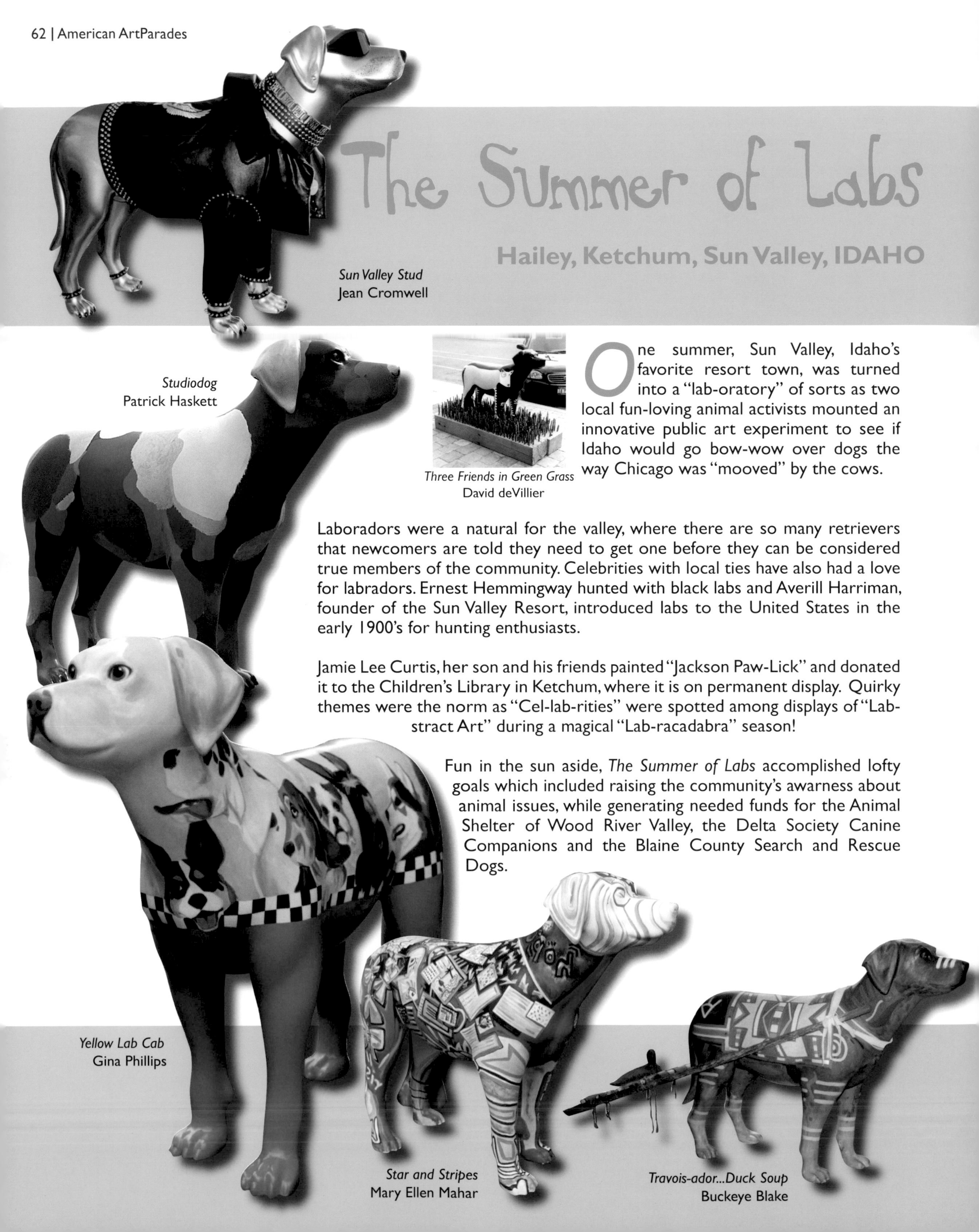

The Summer of Labs

Hailey, Ketchum, Sun Valley, IDAHO

Sun Valley Stud
Jean Cromwell

Studiodog
Patrick Haskett

Three Friends in Green Grass
David deVillier

One summer, Sun Valley, Idaho's favorite resort town, was turned into a "lab-oratory" of sorts as two local fun-loving animal activists mounted an innovative public art experiment to see if Idaho would go bow-wow over dogs the way Chicago was "mooved" by the cows.

Laboradors were a natural for the valley, where there are so many retrievers that newcomers are told they need to get one before they can be considered true members of the community. Celebrities with local ties have also had a love for labradors. Ernest Hemmingway hunted with black labs and Averill Harriman, founder of the Sun Valley Resort, introduced labs to the United States in the early 1900's for hunting enthusiasts.

Jamie Lee Curtis, her son and his friends painted "Jackson Paw-Lick" and donated it to the Children's Library in Ketchum, where it is on permanent display. Quirky themes were the norm as "Cel-lab-rities" were spotted among displays of "Lab-stract Art" during a magical "Lab-racadabra" season!

Fun in the sun aside, *The Summer of Labs* accomplished lofty goals which included raising the community's awarness about animal issues, while generating needed funds for the Animal Shelter of Wood River Valley, the Delta Society Canine Companions and the Blaine County Search and Rescue Dogs.

Yellow Lab Cab
Gina Phillips

Star and Stripes
Mary Ellen Mahar

Travois-ador...Duck Soup
Buckeye Blake

Skylab...the Quest for the Cosmic Milkbone
Randall Brown

"This 'ceLABration' was designed to promote art in the community and enrich the lives of animals and people."

eLABorate on the Wisdom of Animals
Nancy Thomas

Labitat
Mary Roberson

Jackson Paw-Lick
Jamie Lee Curtis, Thomas Guest and friends, Jack and Charlie Wyman

Hot Dog
Carol Glenn

Pilchuck Dumpster Dog
Catherine Rahn

Bearfoot Lab
Debbie Edgers Sturges

Labrador Dali
Martine Drackett

Corn-on-the-Curb Bloomington, Illinois

OP-CORN, Cynthia Shin-Yi Wang

The mighty ear of golden corn was chosen as the symbol of Bloomington, Illinois, to honor its agricultural heritage and rich corn harvests. When the 6-foot tall ears were unveiled on the Fourth of July as part of its Sesquicentennial Celebration, they were greeted with love and smiles. They stood as proud sentinels to hometown humor.

Corn On the Run
Dana Hoback

"Abraham Lincorn" greeted the community, just as the real Abe Lincoln did when he rode the circuit in the mid-1800s. Stand out favorites were "Cornmin Miranda," "Tie Cobb," "Vincent Van d'Ear," and "Coblo Picasso's Corn Maidens." Hands down, the most ambitious ear was "Indian Maize," with over two hundred fifty portraits painted on the kernels. The Bloomington Cultural District was "popping" with joy to be the beneficiary of this golden project.

Tie Cobb, Allison Carr

Totem, Ron Wojanowski

Star-Crossed Pollinators, Herb Eaton

Cornmin Miranda, Harold Gregor

Indian Maize, Ken Holder

" 'Abraham Lincorn'

greeted the community, just as the real Abe Lincoln did when he rode the circuit in the mid-1800s."

Colonel Corn, Mark Blumenshine

Coblo Picasso's Corn Graces, Anne Scott

Abraham Lincorn, Rick Harney

Cows On Parade™ In Chicago

Chicago, Illinois

Bridge Cow, Chris Holt

I Did Not Start the Chicago Fire
Mr. Imagination

Odalisque (Reclining Nude)
Mike Baur

Untitled
Vince Darmody and Michael Langlois

Top Cow, Stan Sczepanski

Cows are certainly an appropriate symbol for Chicago. This city had developed a reputation as the stockyard and railroad center of the Midwest. Legend has it Mrs. O'Leary's cow started the Great Fire of 1871. The mascot for the city's professional basketball team is a bull.

And so it came as no surprise that a Chicago businessman named Peter Hanig returned from his vacation in Zurich, Switzerland with compelling stories about a hugely popular bovine-themed public art event that had created a spectacular Swiss stampede. One thing would lead to another and soon the cows would come home again. This time, they came as an artistic herd that forever changed the notion of public art. This phenomenon was called *Cows on Parade™ In Chicago.*

Waiter, Ken Aiken, Aardvark Studio

"Three hundred fiberglass cows ended up standing, grazing or lying on the streets of Chicago."

Cows On Parade™ In Chicago

Chicago, Illinois

How did it all happen? In what would become the model for cities across the country, a successful private/public partnership between the Chicago Department of Cultural Affairs and the local business community led to a "cattle call" for creative designs from artists and artisans for imaginatively painting and decorating three hundred fiberglass cows that ended up standing, grazing or lying on the streets of Chicago.

With puns for names – "Tutancowmon," "Cowapatra," "Cowleidoscope," "Picowsso," "Mootise," and "Holy Cow" - the herd was a hit. City leaders would estimate that by the end of the cows' reign, after they had been rounded up and auctioned off for charity, they had brought in over $100 million of revenue to the city, while raising over $3.5 million for worthy philanthropic organizations, prompting Mayor Richard Daley to proclaim it "the single largest and most successful event in the history of Chicago."

Hey-diddle-diddle
William McBride with Pat Moss and Michael Stack

Planet Chicowgo
Lois Mrejsa

Grazing with the Cows, George Rodrigue

Modern Family Cow
James Kuhn

Guernsica
Karl Kochvar

Silencing the Birds
Teresa Hofheimer

Palmer House Aristocow
Maryanne Warton

Elmhurst, Illinois

Unlike the many animal themes that were popular in various cities, Elmhurst's icon reflected America's long-standing love affair with automobiles. Twenty-five small-scale, vintage-style, double-seated, Chitty Chitty Bang Bang-type buggies provided the canvas. Designed to be interactive, they had enough natural open air seating for four cool kids to climb aboard.

Gotta Hemi
Berlin Auto Body

The proceeds from the sale of the *Cool Kiddie Cars* went to support the Elmhurst Children's Assistance Foundation.

This spectacular project had enough horsepower left over to fuel future artistic ventures, including *Cool Kiddie Choo Choos* and *Cool Kiddie Tortoises*.

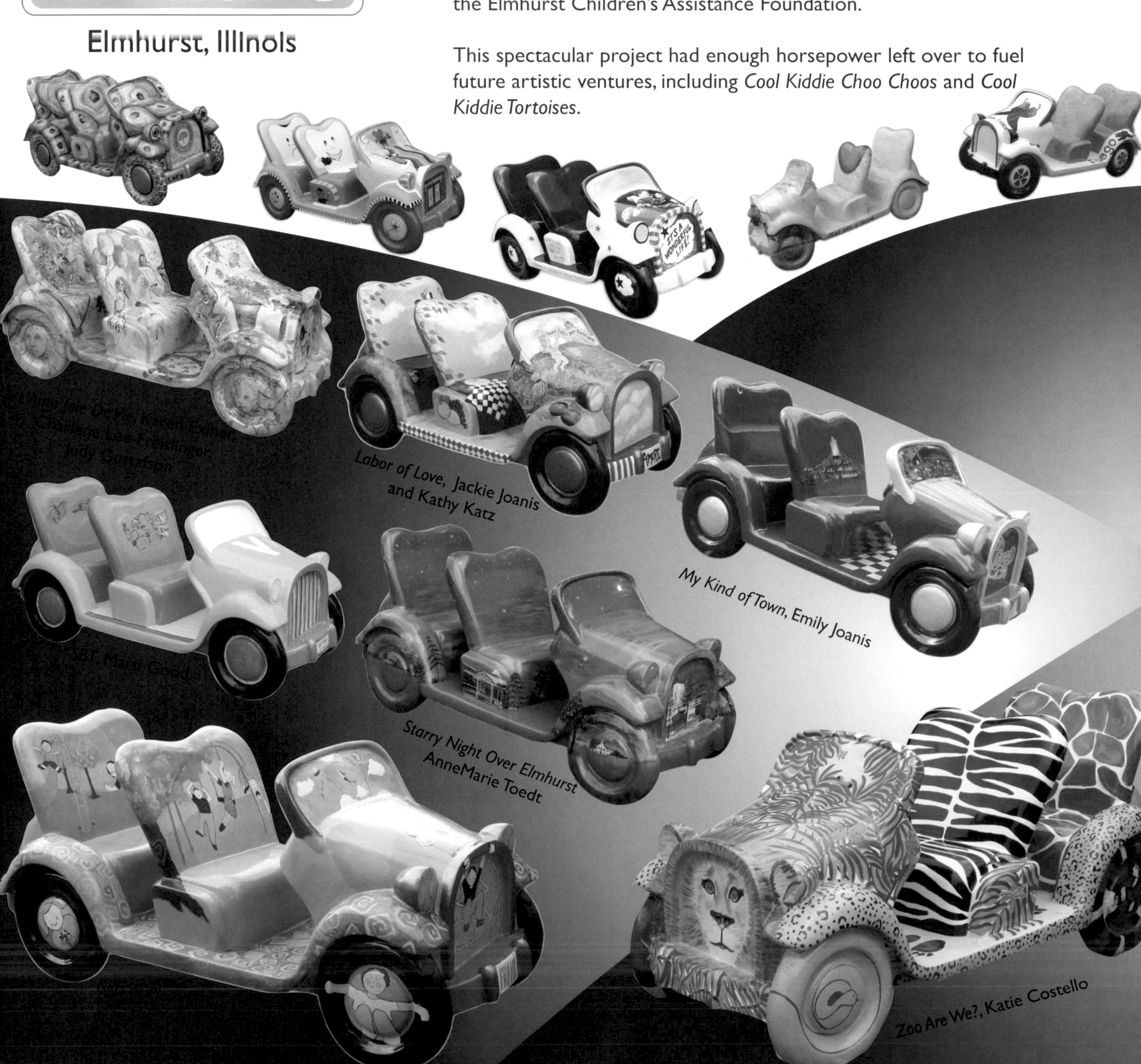

L'Auto Joie De Vie, Karen Exner, Charlene Lee-Freislinger, Judy Gustafson

Labor of Love, Jackie Joanis and Kathy Katz

My Kind of Town, Emily Joanis

SBT, Marci Good

Starry Night Over Elmhurst AnneMarie Toedt

Zoo Are We?, Katie Costello

On The Street of Dreams
Donna Castellanos

"Elmhurst's icon reflected America's long-standing love affair with automobiles."

Images below left to right: *Let's Slow Down*, Donna Castellanos, *Brushing Up Your Smile*, Karen Hanisch, *It's A Wonderful Life*, Terri Gregory, *National Dream*, Debbie Conroy, *Fuego Mobile*, Debbie Conroy, *Wright's Craft Cruiser*, Laura Meyer and Joan Borchert, *California Dreamin'*, Sylvia Mullen, *Peanuts*, Debbie Conroy and Allison Brahm, *Power of Purple*, Katie Kieft, Nicole MacKenzie, Kendall Steffens and B. Szaluga, *Bob Is Building*, Terri Gregory

Childhood Disney
Deb Conroy

Elmhurst's Favorite Dealer
AnneMarie Toedt

Elmhurst Police Paddywagon
Kurt Schiele

Magical Giving Garden; Farmyard Friends

Naperville, Illinois

Most of the communities that caught the public art fever and turned their streets and sidewalks into stages for decorated sculpture focused on a single animal or theme. The Naperville United Way was preparing to celebrate its 50th anniversary and chose to honor this wonderful milestone by mounting a series of extraordinary animal-themed public art exhibitions that proved to be so successful that they continued for five years in a row.

First came giraffes. They were followed by carousel horses, then bears, then farmyard animals and garden sculptures. Along came mushroom houses that sprouted along the Riverwalk while whimsical fairy benches offered resting spots to people strolling downtown. And, if you looked up, you might have noticed the butterflies suspended from the street lamps.

All this culminated with *Mystical Dragons*. Dragons have starred in mythology, folkore and legends for thousands of years. Every country in the world has some sort of dragon story to share. Soon Naperville had its own unique dragon tales to tell and the pot of gold at the end of this rainbow was the $600,000. that was raised to support the Naperville United Way.

Inspiration
Laurie Pollpeter Eskenazi

Jungle Fun
Sue Scholfield

African Sa-Fairy
Kate Gingold

Luminary
Adrianne Subach

Harry's Secret Chamber
Liza Netzley Hopkins

Friends United
Laura Gerardy-Campbell

Bling
Joan Erickson

Ribrest
Laurie Pollpeter Eskenazi

Noble Titania
Natalie McQueen

Lotus Blossom
S. Michael Re

Norman the Banker
Gigi Gentile

Sitting On My Nest Egg
Grace Rosa

Trader Dragon
Lynne Piotrowski

"Along came mushroom houses that sprouted along the Riverwalk while whimsical fairy benches offered resting spots to people strolling downtown."

Patty the Painting Pig
Sue Schofield

Nellie Belle
Jan Dusek

Potter's Place
Cathy J. Bouchard

National Freedom
Kathy Swim

Going to the Chapel
Cherie Matousek

Portabella Playhouse,
Amy White

The Place to Grow
Laura Kilicarslan

Room to Grow
Grace Rosa

Adopt-A-Bee

Zion, Illinois

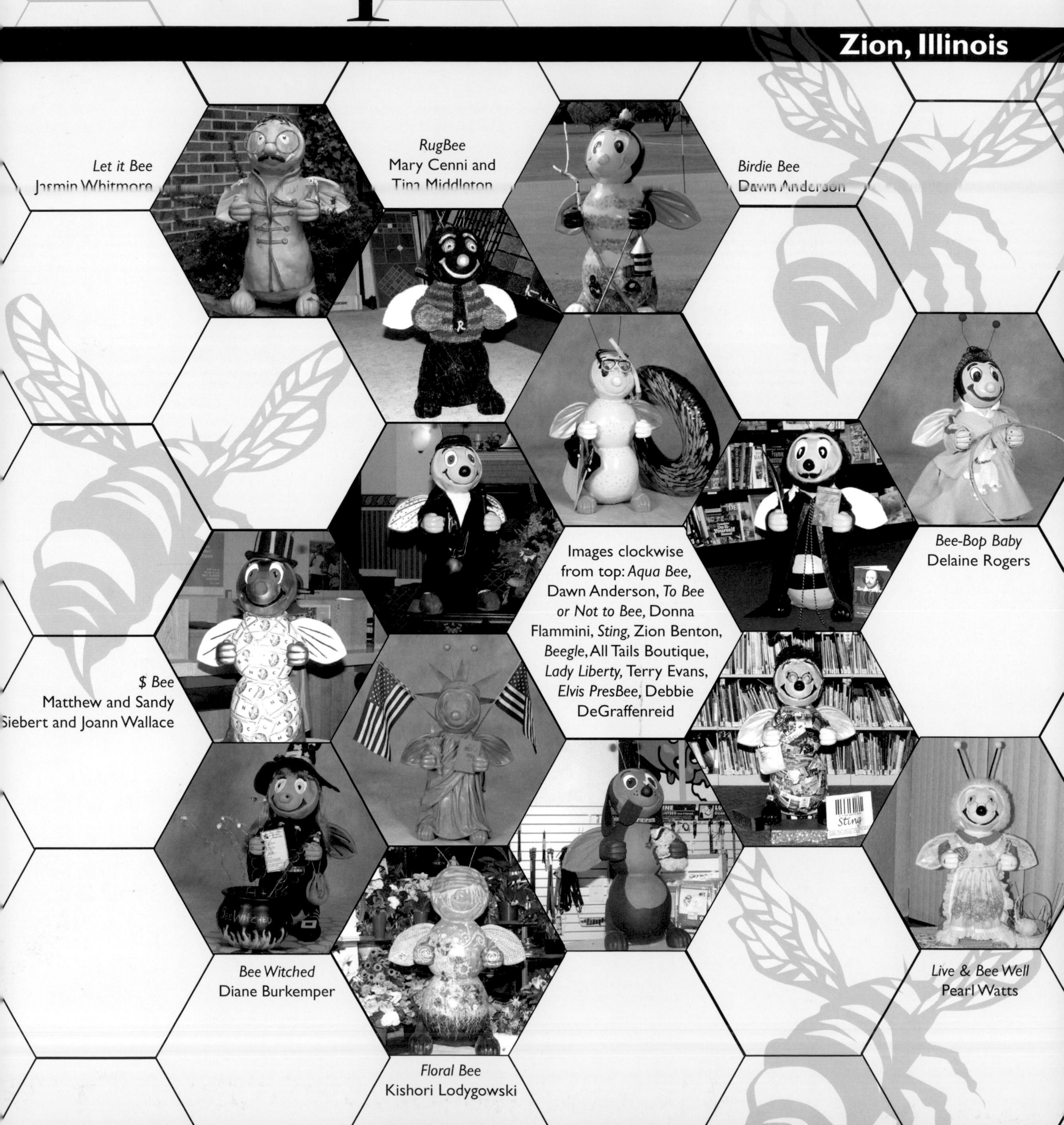

Let it Bee
Jasmin Whitmore

RugBee
Mary Cenni and
Tina Middleton

Birdie Bee
Dawn Anderson

Bee-Bop Baby
Delaine Rogers

Images clockwise from top: *Aqua Bee,* Dawn Anderson, *To Bee or Not to Bee,* Donna Flammini, *Sting,* Zion Benton, *Beegle,* All Tails Boutique, *Lady Liberty,* Terry Evans, *Elvis PresBee,* Debbie DeGraffenreid

$ Bee
Matthew and Sandy
Siebert and Joann Wallace

Bee Witched
Diane Burkemper

Live & Bee Well
Pearl Watts

Floral Bee
Kishori Lodygowski

"This honey of a project has revived our sense of community."

It would be difficult to imagine St. Louis without its classic arch or Orlando without Mickey. For Zion, Illinois, it would be impossible to tell their story without their bees. Indeed, to their knowledge, Zion is the only city with a bee as its official image.

This made the decision easy when it came to selecting a three-dimensional canvas for their animal-themed public art project, and accounts for the community-wide support that greeted *Adopt-A-Bee*. Wearing hospital scrubs, the Mayor and city officials hosted a "bee-livery party" at City Hall. Local business and civic groups sponsored themed representations: The bookstore created "To Bee or Not to Bee," while an auto service business was inspired by John Lennon to create a "Let it Bee" version of the "Bee-tles" song. The city created a "Best of Hive" contest, and purchased an open air trolley that toured people around to the different Bee sculptures. It was christened "The Beeline," of course.

This honey of a project garnered national attention via Good Morning America, the Internet and its own devoted local media. Having recently celebrated its 100th anniversary as a city, the bee-keepers vowed to keep things buzzing for many years to come. The Zion Benton High School Scholarship Fund and the entire city of Zion benefited from the *Adopt-A-Bee* Program.

JuliBee
Diane Burkemper

Rubee the Red Hatter, The Zion Red Hat Society members

BobBee the Builder
Don Stratmoen

Queen Bee
Carla Villalobos

PhotograBee
Carla Villalobos

Fort Wayne, Indiana

MASTODONS ON PARADE

Daisy Don
Thera Bailey

"The mastodons that roamed Indiana thousands of years ago returned, this time as 'mastopieces'."

Thousands of years ago, mastodons roamed northeast Indiana. In the 21st century they returned, this time as 6-foot tall, fiberglass "mastopieces," decked out in styles from grand funk to fine art, from the philosophical to the whimsical.

The project was generated by Indiana University-Purdue University Fort Wayne, as part of the University's 40th anniversary celebration, and two distinguishing features set *Mastodons on Parade* apart from other community art projects: high-tech sound devices allowed each of them to speak, sing or roar: and an original mastodon curriculum was developed and made available to educators.

Mastodons on Parade was wildly successful with one hundred two mammoth sculptures that found their way into the communities heart, as they roared with pride and raised funds to benefit the United Way of Allen County.

Omni Don
University of Saint Francis American Advertising College Chapter

Do it Yourself Don
Do it Best Graphics Department

Don at Work
Kathy Minnich and Michael Bowerman

People at Work Don
Terry Ratliff

Trojan Don
Associates of ICON

AeroDONamic
Lea Ann Gebhand and Ron Mitchell

Dolphins BY DESIGN

Indianapolis, Indiana

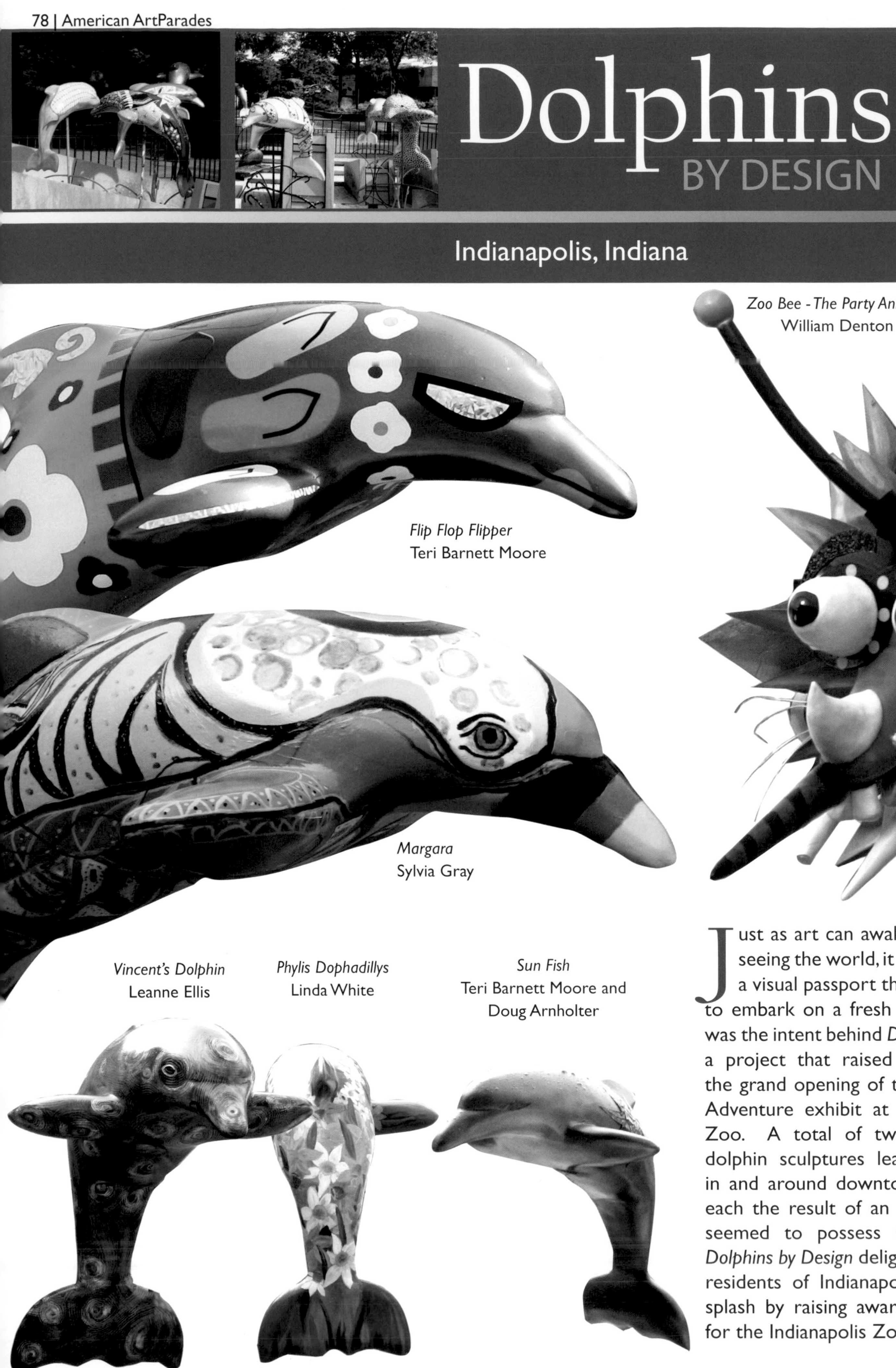

Zoo Bee - The Party Animal
William Denton Ray

Flip Flop Flipper
Teri Barnett Moore

Margara
Sylvia Gray

Vincent's Dolphin
Leanne Ellis

Phylis Dophadillys
Linda White

Sun Fish
Teri Barnett Moore and Doug Arnholter

Just as art can awaken new ways of seeing the world, it can also serve as a visual passport that invites people to embark on a fresh adventure. This was the intent behind *Dolphins by Design*, a project that raised the curtain on the grand opening of the new Dolphin Adventure exhibit at the Indianapolis Zoo. A total of twenty, 5-foot tall dolphin sculptures leapt into the air, in and around downtown Indianapolis, each the result of an imagination that seemed to possess magical powers. *Dolphins by Design* delighted visitors and residents of Indianapolis, and made a splash by raising awareness and funds for the Indianapolis Zoo.

"Dolphin sculptures leapt into the air, each the result of an imagination that seemed to possess magical powers."

Flapper, Sheila Jackson

Reflections on a Moonlit Night
Carrie Claycomb

Harvey Harlequin, Clown of the Sea
Teri Barnett Moore

Pablony Phincasso-Secret Ingredient
William Denton Ray

Pippin, the Painted Pony
Harmonyx

Overalls All Over

"An American Gothic Happening"

Cedar Rapids, Iowa

Cedar Rapids has a special connection to the artist Grant Wood, who achieved worldwide recognition with his painting titled "American Gothic," which posed a stiff Midwestern farmer wearing overalls beside his strait-laced sister in front of a two-story house with a pointed Gothic-style window. He was their native son, a teacher in their schools, decorator of area homes, in addition to being the creator of the most copied and caricatured image in American art today.

"The gift Grant Wood shared with us was the ability to look in our own backyard and find a world of things worth celebrating," became the moral behind *Overalls All Over*, a project that showcased a series of American Gothic statues throughout the downtown area that were intended to celebrate his colorful legacy and educate visitors about the impact of Wood's contribution to American art.

Overalls Lost When Tech Stocks Tanked
Catherine Jones Davies, Tech Advisers,
Lynn and Everett Russell

He Wooden Smile, and Neither Wood She, Jeff Gnagy

Wood in Wood, Karla McGrail

Prairie Gothic Blues, Carol Macomber

Cone and Wood, Peter Thompson

Under the Sea-der: Amerifin Gothic, Three Arts Creative Team

Fields and Dreams, Dana Noble

"The gift Grant Wood shared with us was the ability to look in our own backyard and find a world of things worth celebrating."

Prairie Dog Quest

sioux city art center

Sioux City, Iowa

"The *Prairie Dog Quest* was initiated to promote art, civic pride, tourism and Siouxland's prominence in the Lewis and Clark Bicentennial."

Large images below, left to right: *Prairiewether Lewis & William-Dog Clark*, Paul N. Chelstad and Nan E. Wilson, *Gumball*, Arthur Georgopoulos, *Prairie Dog Days, A River Runs Through It*, Linda Wooten-Green, *Prairie Doordog*, Rita M. Habeger, *Buckskin Floyd,* Michael Hobbs, *Corn Dog*, Brenda Schoenherr-Thelen, *Little House on the Prairie Dog*, Linda Wooten-Green, *Prairiewether Lewis & William*, Paul N. Chelstad and Nan E. Wilson

As Lewis and Clark explored the grasslands of the Midwest in 1804, they encountered thousands of dirt mounds inhabited by what they called "barking squirrels." This strange sight was difficult to explain, so the explorers decided to capture one of these unusual creatures and send it to President Jefferson. A boat ride down the Mississippi River to New Orleans, a ship trip to Baltimore, and a wagon ride to Washington, DC later, this special little prairie dog charmed an amused President.

With this legacy in mind, the Sioux City Art Center decided to mount a public art project showcasing artistic interpretations of the animal that was symbolic of the Lewis and Clark Expedition, and Siouxland's place in that landmark journey. *Prairie Dog Quest* left a lasting mark, strengthening the community's commitment to making art accessible to all people and promoting civic pride in the community, while inspiring residents and visitors to learn more about the amazing story of Lewis and Clark and the Corps of Discovery.

Sioux City, Iowa

So popular was the *Prairie Dog Quest* public art project, that the Sioux City Art Center developed *Discovery Dog*. These playful dogs were inspired by "Seaman," the intrepid Newfoundland dog that accompanied Lewis and Clark on their historic journey. They spent five months on the streets of Sioux City and found permanent homes after a live auction at the Art Center. Even today, the decorated dogs can be found proudly displayed on street corners, in bank lobbies and in front of businesses throughout the tri-state community.

"Distinctive and delightful, personable and playful, Newfoundland dogs took their places on the landscape of Siouxland."

Left page large images, left to right: *Discovery of Refreshment*, Andrea Phillips, *Security Dog*, Netha Wise, *The Ringmaster*, Ray Monlux
This page large images, left to right: *Hot Fudge Hound*, Nan Wilson, *Hustler Dog*, Brenda Schoenherr-Thelen, *Sentinel of the Prairie*, Deb Gengler Copple

Louisville, Kentucky

Images left to right:
Oopsie Daisy, Frank Perrone,
Ben Ali 'The Greatest', Joe Weber,
Bae Bae, N. Travis King

Thunder Gulch, Linda Barnett, Bits & Pieces

Home of the Kentucky Derby – the greatest two minutes in sports – Louisville naturally selected horses as their "canvas" and as a way of paying tribute to the race and the festival surrounding it. Artists were encouraged to create a design based on the name or the year a famous racehorse won the garland of roses.

A wide variety of media were used to embellish the sculptures, from candy to commemorative pins, ceramic dishes to stained glass, copper strands to cotton fabric, pine needles to tissue paper, and everything in between. The results became Louisville's Sidewalk Derby.

Gallopalooza featured over two hundred decorated thoroughbreds throughout the entire community, as well as Southern Indiana. When "the race" was finished, $500,000. had been raised for local charities and Brightside, the city's beautification program.

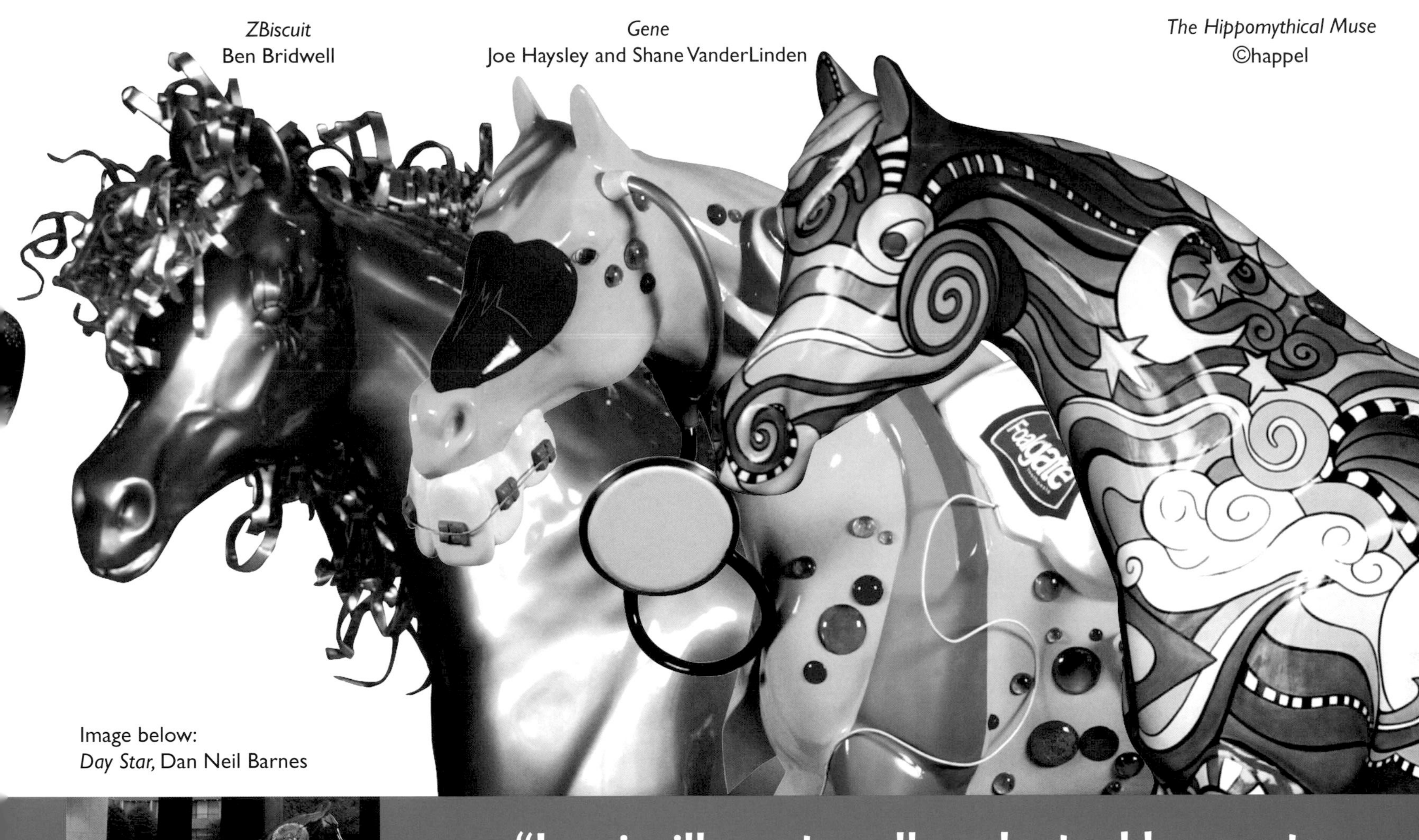

ZBiscuit
Ben Bridwell

Gene
Joe Haysley and Shane VanderLinden

The Hippomythical Muse
©happel

Image below:
Day Star, Dan Neil Barnes

“Louisville naturally selected horses to pay tribute to the race and festival surrounding it.”

Images below from left: *Pink Star,* Kathleen Buckowski-Ritter, *Venetian Way ‘Grandiloquent’,* Bartholomew A. Herre, *Sunny’s Halo ‘The Winning Purse’,* Doreen Barnhart DeHart, *Schmipff’s Candy Dapple*, Susan Jill Hedges, *Smarty Jones ‘Soaring’,* Robert and Robin Tillman

Shiver Me Timbers, Judy B. Patterson

gators ON THE geaux

Lake Charles, Louisiana

An "outdoor museum" was created in Southwest Louisiana when over one hundred decorated, larger than life alligators were displayed on the streets and in the businesses of Lake Charles. Who would have suspected that the word "gator" could inspire so many different interpretations? "In-Vest-A–Gator", "Tail Gator", "Irrigator", "Navigator", "Roman Gladi-Gator", "Litigator", "Ed-U-Gator." A lover of the swamps, the alligator is the quintessential symbol of this part of the country.

Local Lendigator, Susan Arnold Fuerst

The Lake Charles Symphony and The Arts and Humanities Council of Southwest Louisiana were delighted to introduce *Gators on the Geaux*, one of the most remarkable events Southwest Louisiana has ever experienced. The Lake Charles Symphony was swamped with community and financial support, and was the beneficiary of this extraordinary project, a striking example of art helping art.

See You Later Alligator
Fred Stark

Gatorbait
Lawrence Rybicki and Lewis Temple

Senator Gator
Felix Falgoust

Unnamed
Fred Stark

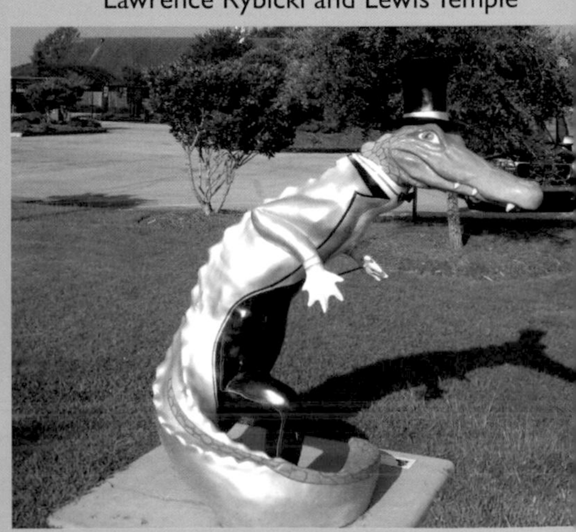

Kurt E. C. Gator
Fred Stark

Amerigator, Leigh Rush

Safety Gator, Judy B. Patterson

Art-A-Gator, Susan Arnold Fuerst

"Rising out of the swamps came the gator - that quintessential Southwest Louisiana symbol."

Tail Gator
Lawrence Rybicki and Lewis Temple

Gospel Gator
Julie Pumpelly

Cajun Country
David Reed II

Litigator
Anne L. Dentler

Illumigator
Stephen M. Madden and Shawna Nile Batchelor

Ed Drew Gator
Susan Arnold Fuerst

Belfast Bearfest

Belfast, Maine

Bearly Enough Time
Kimber Lee Clark and Scott Sebold

"It rises like a skateboard slope from the shores of Penobscot Bay and, yes, this small city was home to the first roller-skating rink in the country, so maybe it makes sense that a bear is wearing roller skates downtown," began the article in the Boston Globe newspaper. "But what about the bear dressed as a rooster? How do you explain that?" How else but *Belfast Bearfest*, northern New England's first entry into the national public art sweepstakes.

The Mayor of Belfast, Maine, Mike Hurley, was visiting Chicago in the summer of 1999 and experienced *Cows on Parade,* the city-wide public art project. He was so excited about this spectacular exhibition and knew immediately that he would bring this idea home to Belfast.

This coastal community is known for many things, and bears are certainly one of them. With their large bodies, and smooth round surfaces, they turned out to be the perfect choice for this offbeat artfest. Billed as the largest exhibition of outdoor art ever to hit Maine, *Belfast Bearfest* demonstrated the social, economic and artistic value of community art exhibitions and went on to become an annual festival for the next three years. This award-winning public art project generated national media attention and the proceeds from the auction of these bears supported local non-profit organizations.

Face It, John Balzer

Ursa, Rebecca McCall

Froggy, David Hurley and Ken Oberholtzer

Aurora Bearalis, Alan Fishman

"The Maine Tourism Association awarded the *Belfast Bearfest* with the top award for Special Events."

A Circus Bear, Stu Henderson

Left to right: *American Bearlines,* William C. Klausmeyer, *Bearielle, The Passy Merbear,* Susan Tobey White, *Admiral Ray Dresses Up and Goes Out with the Chickens,* Rick Cronin, *Four Seasons Bear,* Annie Earhart Gray

Images above right corner, clockwise: *Spoon-A*, Jim Opasik, *Monk Fish*, Courtney Sinn, *Carefirst Bluefish*, Steven Hammer, *Cone Fish*, Kristin Helberg, *Divine Fish Out of Waters*, Anthea Zeltzman, *Shark Lark*, Anthony Cervino

Baltimore, Maryland

Hooked on Technology
Laurie Levitt and
Connie Matricardi

"The rainbow-colored, rhinestone-encrusted fish made a big splash."

Images above left corner, clockwise: *Walking Fish*, Ming Yi Sung, *Florentina*, Dorothy Fix, *Water Taxi*, Mike Anthony and Sarah Barnes, *Pesce di Vetro*, Anthony Coradetti, *The Rock Garden*, Rufus Toomey, *Still Life*, Phyllis Saroff, *Angel Fish*, Betty Schroll, *Allure of Baltimore*, Mike Anthony and Sarah Barnes
Center image: *Aloha Mahi Mahi*, Lisa Hutton

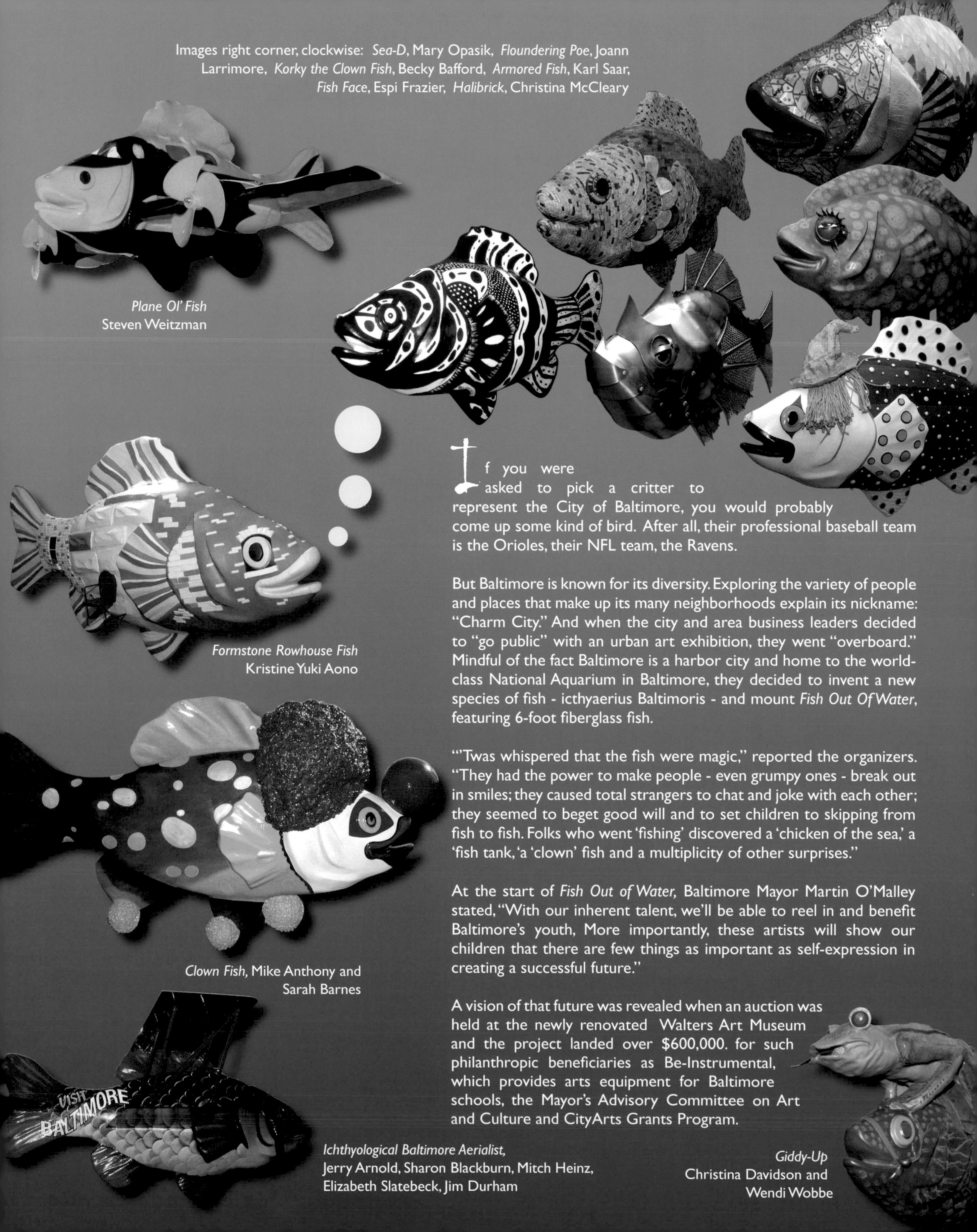

Images right corner, clockwise: *Sea-D*, Mary Opasik, *Floundering Poe*, Joann Larrimore, *Korky the Clown Fish*, Becky Bafford, *Armored Fish*, Karl Saar, *Fish Face*, Espi Frazier, *Halibrick*, Christina McCleary

Plane Ol' Fish
Steven Weitzman

Formstone Rowhouse Fish
Kristine Yuki Aono

Clown Fish, Mike Anthony and Sarah Barnes

Ichthyological Baltimore Aerialist,
Jerry Arnold, Sharon Blackburn, Mitch Heinz, Elizabeth Slatebeck, Jim Durham

Giddy-Up
Christina Davidson and Wendi Wobbe

If you were asked to pick a critter to represent the City of Baltimore, you would probably come up some kind of bird. After all, their professional baseball team is the Orioles, their NFL team, the Ravens.

But Baltimore is known for its diversity. Exploring the variety of people and places that make up its many neighborhoods explain its nickname: "Charm City." And when the city and area business leaders decided to "go public" with an urban art exhibition, they went "overboard." Mindful of the fact Baltimore is a harbor city and home to the world-class National Aquarium in Baltimore, they decided to invent a new species of fish - icthyaerius Baltimoris - and mount *Fish Out Of Water*, featuring 6-foot fiberglass fish.

"'Twas whispered that the fish were magic," reported the organizers. "They had the power to make people - even grumpy ones - break out in smiles; they caused total strangers to chat and joke with each other; they seemed to beget good will and to set children to skipping from fish to fish. Folks who went 'fishing' discovered a 'chicken of the sea,' a 'fish tank,'a 'clown' fish and a multiplicity of other surprises."

At the start of *Fish Out of Water,* Baltimore Mayor Martin O'Malley stated, "With our inherent talent, we'll be able to reel in and benefit Baltimore's youth, More importantly, these artists will show our children that there are few things as important as self-expression in creating a successful future."

A vision of that future was revealed when an auction was held at the newly renovated Walters Art Museum and the project landed over $600,000. for such philanthropic beneficiaries as Be-Instrumental, which provides arts equipment for Baltimore schools, the Mayor's Advisory Committee on Art and Culture and CityArts Grants Program.

LIVINGSTON COUNTY HABITAT FOR HUMANITY®
FUNDRAISER

Animal House

Brighton
Howell
MICHIGAN

"Rain" Deer
Betsy McDaniel

Of Africa
Michele Anscombe

What do lions, tigers, giraffes, and horses have in common? What kind of habitat would accommodate such a diverse collection of creatures? You would know the answer if you had taken a walk on the wild side of Howell and Brighton, Michigan the year it was taken over by the public art project, *Animal House*.

Images left to right: *Ciabella de Colores (Horse of Colors),* Sara Hunter, *Patriot,* Nancy Kern, *Night & Day,* Erik Reichenback, *Leonardo,* Colleen Cowhy

"Take a walk on the wild side."

Images left to right, top to bottom: *The "King,"* Diane Tasselmyer, *Art Beast,* Howell High School Art Students, James Van Coppenolle, Instructor, *Jake "The Smooth Jazz Man,"*, Jeff Spade, *Graceful Girt,* Gail Sanchirico, *Dande-Lion,* Lea Kucharek, *Sea Lion,* Jerry Hosier

Light House Bear
Laura Williams and
Brighton Women's Camp

LIVINGSTON COUNTY HABITAT FOR HUMANITY®
FUNDRAISER

The Bear Necessities

Brighton, Fowlerville, Howell and Pinckney
MICHIGAN

Tommy Bahama
Diane Tasselmyer

Grin and "Bear" it
Nancy Gray

The Nosey Neigh-Bear
Leah Kucharek

So successful was *Animal House* that Brighton and Howell, Michigan decided to put on a second project the following year and two new communites, Pinckney and Fowlerville, joined the fun. And this time, extravagantly painted bears roamed through Livingston County. *The Bear Necessities* appropriately benefited the Livingston County Habitat for Humanity® and Habitat International's Hurricane Katrina Relief Effort.

Bearly Caring
James Van Coppenolle

Pirate E. Bear
Deborah Scharp

Saint Andrew
Diane Tasselmyer

Dr. Fuz E. Bear
Kelly Cousino

Northern Spirit
Mark Thompson

A Beary Good Day
Kimberly Holback

Hula Bear
Gayle Sanchirico

Botanical Bear
Pamela Stoddard

Frogs • Fur • Friends

Grosse Pointe, Michigan

Lord Frogerick, John Furkin

There are one hundred and seventy species of poisonous frogs living in the rainforests of Central and South America. Many are brightly colored to warn predators to stay away. The fifty-three, 54-inch high, 50-pound, fiberglass amphibious critters that hopped, crouched and leapt up and down the streets of Grosse Pointe, Michigan were equally as colorful. But instead of bringing danger to the community, they were a ribbitting attraction with a happily-ever-after ending.

The waterfront location of the Pointes, along with the historic marshland and ribbon of farms, made the frogs the natural choice for the fun and fanciful sculptures that both amazed and amused.

Frogs • Fur • Friends was a fairy tale indeed. After expenses, it had raised $250,000. for The Childrens Home of Detroit and the Grosse Pointe Animal Adoption Society.

Flora, Tim Marsh

Bull Frog, Mike Chrumka

Dig It!, Michael Stapleton/Avanti Press

Images left to right: *Money Frog,* William Johnston, *Maizen Blu,* Hugh O'Connor, *Sparty,* Mike Stapleton, *Peaceable Kingdom,* Susan Bolt

"The frogs were a ribbitting attraction with a happily-ever-after ending."

Commodore Boll Frog, Christine Codish

Frog Flux, Nina Goebel

Art on the Frog, Ann Baxter

Leap for the Stars, Nancy Pitel

Images left to right: *Tour de Frog,* Nance Aitchison, *Hot Frogger,* Gregory Cheesewright, *Leaperace (Leap er a chee),* Pamela Ahee Thomas and Michael Stapleton, *Fly Fish'n Frog,* Ken Wiktor

THE EWE REVUE

Rochester, Michigan

Most of the successful public art events were designed around an animal that played a pivotal role in the community's history. Rochester, Michigan used their project to tell the story of its rich sheep history.

It is a tale with farms and mills at its center: the wool produced by Rochester sheep farmers was processed at mills that, in their time, were among the largest producers of woolen gloves, mittens and lumberman's socks in the world. It is a tale that celebrates the history, pride and spirit of this community with "be-ewe-tiful" sheep sporting such catchy names as: "Ewe Are Here," "Ewe-nity" and "Ewe Go Girl."

Nearly one hundred decorated fiberglass sheep grazed through the landscape of downtown Rochester. *The Ewe Revue* was a community-wide public art event sponsored by the Rochester Downtown Development Authority, benefiting local Rochester charities.

> "The Ewe Revue celebrated the history, pride and spirit of this community with 'be-ewe-tiful' sheep..."

Ewe Should Build Something New
Kelly Sekerak and William Thomas

The Material Ewe, Carol Diehl

Lamb Armstrong, The Staff of WaHu! Bicycle Company

Shasta, Elise Mitzel

When Ewes Fly, Judith Peebles

Car-ewe-sel, Gail Waterous

L-Ewe-Au, Lori Solymosi

Ewe Go Girl, Connie Korach

Beautiful, Beautiful Ewe, Juliana and Cindy Newhou

Lamb Chopper, Ron Finch

Sheep In Wolf's Clothing, Michael Stapleton

Ewe-nicorn, Debi [illegible]

St. Paul's Tribute To Charles M. Schulz

St. Paul, Minnesota

When Charles Schulz announced his retirement, people in St. Paul immediately started discussing ways to honor him. After serious consideration and input from the community, *Peanuts on Parade* was launched. Over one hundred sculptures of Snoopy, painted by local artists, romped across the St. Paul landscape.

Because of its enormous success, the momentum continued with *Charlie Brown Around Town* which gave Minnesota families and visitors another memorable Charles Schultz experience. *Looking For Lucy* marked the third year of St. Paul's tribute to Schulz. And in the fourth year, adorable PEANUTS characters blanketed the streets of St. Paul in *Linus Blankets St. Paul*. *The Doghouse Days of Summer* marked the fifth and final exhibition and featured the classic pose of Snoopy lying on top of his doghouse, daydreaming with his closest friend and confidant Woodstock. Charles Schulz's hometown of St. Paul will always remember him with a smile.

Gumball Snoopy, Rurik

Below from left: *Sunburned Charlie*, Troy Olin, *Snoopy's Christmas Dog House*, John B. Johnson, *I Love Lucy*, Randi Johnson

CHARLIE BROWN AROUND TOWN
SAINT PAUL'S TRIBUTE TO CHARLES M. SCHULZ

LINUS BLANKETS SAINT PAUL
SAINT PAUL'S TRIBUTE TO CHARLES M. SCHULZ

Sincerity In St. Paul, Lindsey Schulz

Jumpin' For Joy, Randi Johnson

"Thank you Charles Schulz for bringing happiness to St. Paul and the world!"

The Doctor Is In
Roy and Lisa Schleztbaum

St. Paul's Tribute To Charles M. Schulz

St. Paul, Minnesota

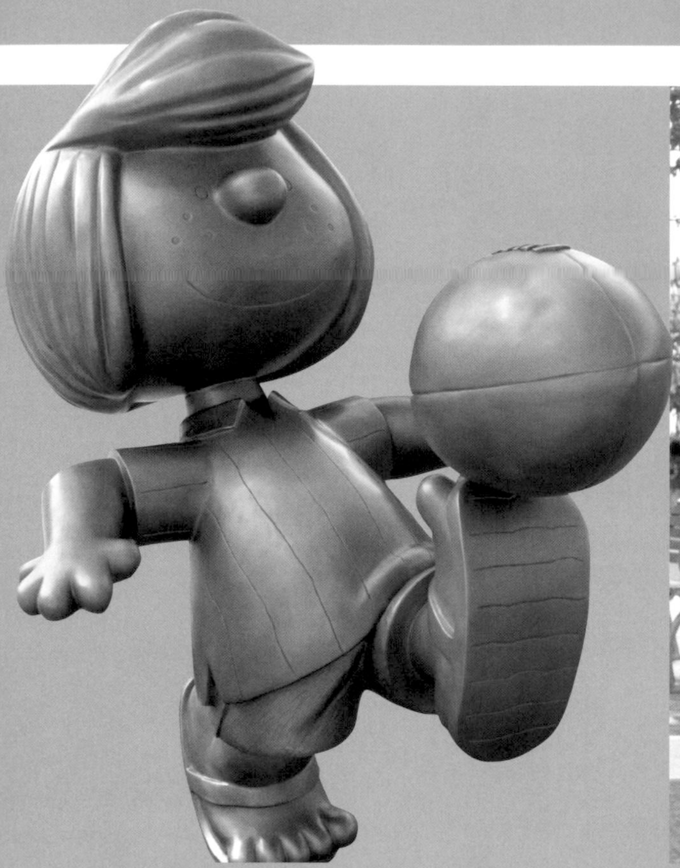

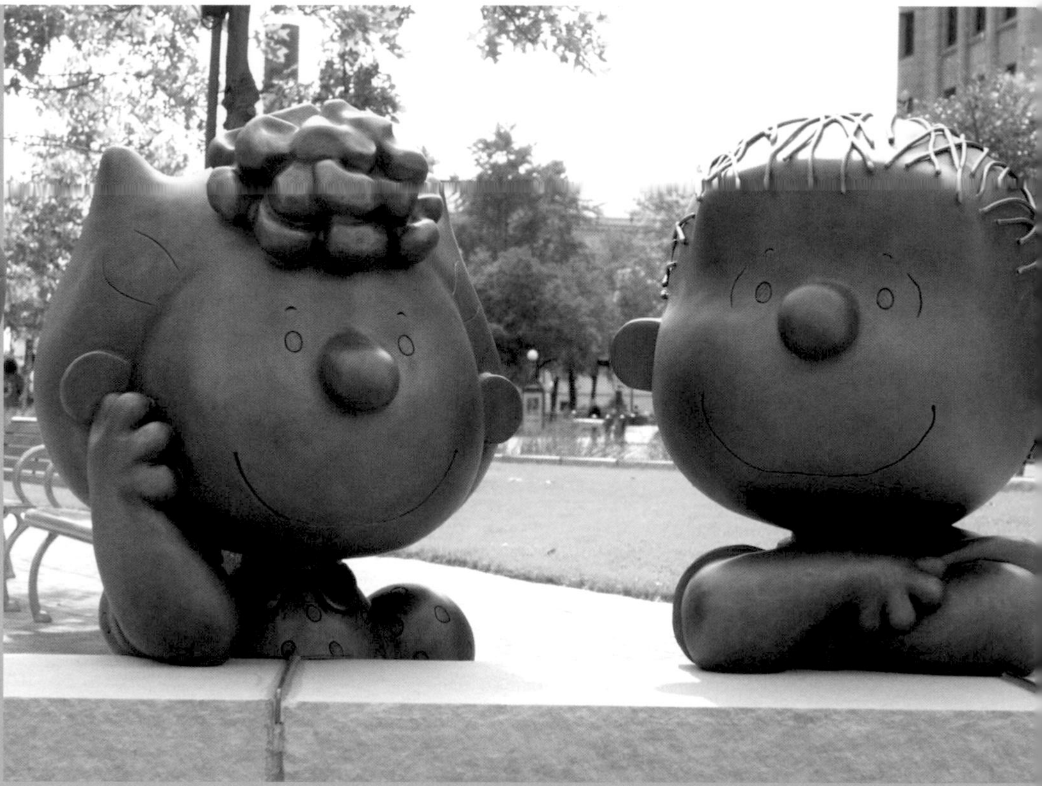

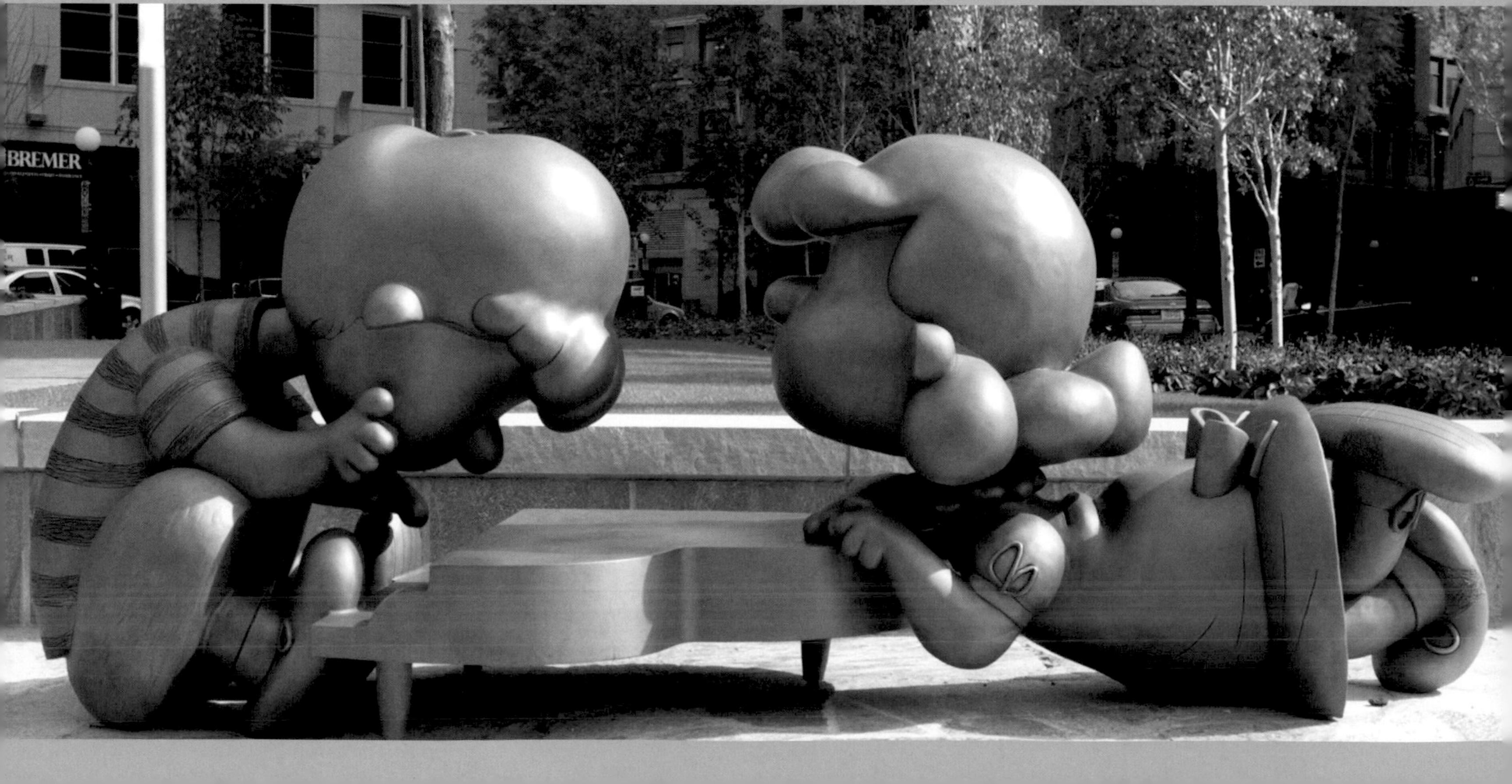

EANUTS ON PARADE
T PAUL'S TRIBUTE TO CHARLES M. SCHULZ

CHARLIE BROWN AROUND TOWN
SAINT PAUL'S TRIBUTE TO CHARLES M. SCHULZ

LINUS BLANKETS SAINT PAUL
SAINT PAUL'S TRIBUTE TO CHARLES M. SCHULZ

DOGHOUSE DAYS OF SUMMER
SAINT PAUL'S TRIBUTE TO CHARLES M. SCHULZ

"Snoopy, Charlie Brown, Linus, Lucy and the Gang demonstrated St. Paul's love for Schulz."

Over three million visitors from all fifty states and over sixty countries around the world, traveled to St. Paul to see and celebrate the PEANUTS personalities with whom they had become so familiar. All truly felt like part of the family. And that is just the way St. Paul and Charles Schulz wanted it to be…

Permanent bronze sculptures of some of the PEANUTS Gang are featured throughout parks in downtown St. Paul for the entire community and the world to enjoy. The City of St. Paul and Capital City Partnership presented the Schulz Tribute Projects whose proceeds went to The Charles M. Schulz Fund to establish scholarships for artists and emerging cartoonists at the Art Instruction School where Schulz attended and taught, as well as the College of Visual Arts.

Above from left: *Happiness Is...*, TivoliToo, Inc., *Charlie Brown visits the "Relay For Life" Event*
Below from left: *Looking For Lucy Artist Paint-Off Event*, *On The Town*, Chuck Gonzales

around town CAROUSELS abound

Meridian, Mississippi

One hears the slogan "History is the start of the future" a lot in Meridian, a strategically located Confederate stronghold during the Civil War that was all but burned to the ground by General William Tecumseh Sherman, who is reputed to have said, "Meridian no longer exists." But the town roared back to life, growing into a landmark in the New South and distinguishing itself further when it became the first city in Mississippi to join the national animals-on-parade phenomenon.

Since Meridian is home to our nation's last original Dentzel Carousel, it made perfect sense that carousel horses were selected as the community icon. Sixty-two horses were "groomed" by local artists, herded through the city, and stood as proud reminders of the imaginative spirit of childhood. Just as an adult lifts a child onto a carousel horse, so too did this project lift the children of Mississippi onto a road of hope.

Around Town Carousels Abound created community pride and an appreciation for art with all of the proceeds benefitting the Hope Village for Children in Meridian.

Bulldog to a Degree
Todd Eldridge

Images above, left to right: *Fantasy Philly*, Jessie Brashier, *Brothers Keeper*, Dottie Armstrong, *Front Street Phoenix*, J. Scott Gavin, *Lightning*, Cathy Castleberry, *Racing for Hope*, Terri Ann Province, *I Spy*, Gail Crawford

Ebony Pride, Ronnie McDowell

Lady, Shannon Norton Everett

"Just as an adult lifts a child onto a carousel horse, so too did this project lift the children of Mississippi onto a road of hope."

Images above, left to right: *Giddy-Up Van Gogh*, Dave Kimbrell, *Fair Lady*, Jane Kynerd, *Horseplay*, Pegi Harmon and Lamar Art Students, *Homestead Horse*, Bryce Speed, *Caretaker*, Bobby Carter

St. Louis, Missouri

Family, the Spirit of St. Louis
Chuck Niesen

Splish Splash
Rich Brooks

Accidental Tourist
Michael Kilfoy and Studio X

Makin' Time
Angela Hunter-Knight

Marina the Mermaid
Robin Murez

In St. Louis a call went out to area residents to submit their suggestions for the type of symbolic "character" they thought best represented the region. After reviewing over 1,200 letters, e-mails and faxes, it was clear that it was the people who made the St. Louis region great… and *The People Project* was conceived.

All the sponsored artists were given adult or child-sized wooden mannequins to act as the structural frames for their figures. Their first task was to pose the mannequin according to the proposed design. Because the mannequins had moveable joints, artists were able to be extremely imaginative in how figures were posed. Individual inventiveness and creativity helped define and heighten the unique character of each piece. Some figures stood solidly on both feet, emphasizing a sense of pride. Other compositions were dramatically balanced on one leg, one arm or a tilted chair. Figures kicked, crouched, knelt, reclined, sat on benches, bikes, stairs and celestial objects. Dynamic poses conveyed a sense of movement, and energized figures ran a gamut of activities – jogging, swimming, surfing, dancing, juggling, roller skating, skateboarding, playing tennis, riding bikes, and even flying.

Nearly 240 years ago, St. Louis was a gateway for our nation's westward expansion. Fast forward to the metropolitan St. Louis of the 21st century and you have a city rich in history and full of imagination, as gloriously illustrated by the one hundred seventy-one works of art featured in *The People Project.* The St. Louis Regional Arts Commission and FOCUS St. Louis developed this project to promote the arts and to raise funds for the Regional Arts Foundation and numerous charities selected by the sponsors.

"It was clear that it was the people who made the St. Louis region great...and The People Project was born."
He's A Real Puzzler
Susan C. Koen
St. Louis Plays
Robert A. Ketchens
Undercover
Kuumba
(Katrin Butler-Powell)
Looking Out Onto The Future
Jan Brander-Kinnison
I Wanna Be A Cowboy
Raphael DiLuzio
Under Standing
Jane Saunders
Impossible Standman
Dennis Syberg
Body Art
Cheryl A. Sander

Cranes on Parade

Kearney, Nebraska

"Cranes are charismatic and social birds."

Roots of Nebraska
Celeste Schulte

Take Five
Jan Smolik

Mirage
Tim, Ivy and Joe Hanson and Kenwood Elementary

It's been written that "There is a magical time that occurs each year in the heart of North America, when the river and the season and the birds all come into brief conjunction."

Each spring, the central Platte River Valley hosts the largest gathering of migratory birds in the world. Millions of ducks and geese, shorebirds, songbirds, and Sandhill Cranes come to feed in the wet meadows along the river. Cranes are charismatic and social birds, standing up to 4-feet high with a 6-foot wingspan. They engage in energetic courtship, dancing and bonding rituals, and they also mate for life. When Kearney decided to join the "animal art movement," there was never a question which regional icon would be selected.

Cranes on Parade demonstrated what a community can do when it cultivates and inspires the art, business and education worlds to work together to accomplish a common goal. Thanks to the efforts of the Kearney Dawn Rotary Club and a tireless group of volunteers, this inspiring public art project raised funds for community service organizations in Kearney and Rotary projects throughout the world.

Carousel Crane
Gary Zaruba

U–Crane
Greg Holdren

Flower Power
Martha Pettigrew

Abbie's Dance
MONA Art Class

Birds on the Horizon
Cecilia Richardson
and Kelli Jo Risk

Old Glory
Larry Peterson

Nature's Eloquence
Donna Knapp

Fossil In Evolution
Roberto Gutierrez

From left to right: *Balances*, Dang Nimchanya, *Fractional Crane*, John Fronczak, *Kearney History Crane*, Brad Norton, *Kaleidoscopic Crane*, David Wiebe, *Kiss of the Platte*, Rivkah Addy, *Klimt on Crane*, Molly Anderson, *A Season Under Heaven*, Pat Wiederspan Jones, Crane Lilly, *Platte River Messenger of the Valley*, Mary Ruff, *Corn Princess*, Cynthia Taylor Lightner, *"Cent"-sational Banking*, Various Artists, *The Promise*, Carol Sanders

From left to right: *Migrating Crane*, Carolyn Jacobsen, *Quilted Crane*, Deborah Sinclair, *Crane Voices*, Arthur Pierce, *'Crane-Berry' & Apple Pie*, Kim Meister, *Craning to See*, Deborah Sinclair, *Sunday Best*, Jennifer Homan, *Business as Usual*, Jennifer Homan, *Crane Illusion*, Prewitt Fiberglass Animals, *Spotted Crane*, Bob Coonts, *Bronze Crane*, Martha Pettigrew, *Buffalo Crane*, Mark Adams

CHAIR-I-TY
Reno, Nevada
"We're talking about those humble, oak, study chairs that went out of fashion in classrooms decades ago and were reincarnated as 'objets d'art.'"
T
Time is...
Too slow for those who wait,
Too swift for those who fear,
Too long for those who grieve,
Too short for those who rejoice,
But for those who love...
Time is Eternity.
Living well and beautifully and justly are all one thing

Lighthouse LobStars & The Lighthouse Kids

North Hampton, New Hampshire

On a warm spring day, a group of seventh graders doing a beach clean up in North Hampton, New Hampshire admired the view of a string of offshore islands known as the Isles of Shoals and the beautiful White Island Lighthouse, 10-miles off the coast of Portsmouth. An important part of the scenic landscape, the lighthouses were a constant reminder of a long history with the sea and a beacon of safety - keeping innumerable boats out of harm's way since the 1860's. A devoted science teacher explained to the students that the White Island Lighthouse on the southernmost island would soon collapse if someone didn't do something soon to save it. "Why don't we do something?" asked one of her students. And so the concept of the Lighthouse Kids was conceived.

Through the years, over two hundred fifty students from the North Hampton School have been involved in various fundraising efforts, culminating in the *Lighthouse LobStars* - a public art project that sprinkled the greater seacoast from Kittery, Maine to Hampton Beach, New Hampshire, with 4-foot tall, fantastically decorated lobster sculptures that were eventually sold to benefit White Island Lighthouse, save it from ruin, and restore it to its former glory.

Along the way, the Lighthouse Kids have learned valuable lessons about the power of art and the importance of historic preservation, which makes communities and lives a little bit richer.

"The Lighthouse Kids have learned valuable lessons about the power of art to make communities and lives a little bit richer."

Images above from left: *Craysea Payslea,* Lynda Kodwyck, *Lobstourist,* Lin Albertson-Thorpe, *Flamin Glory,* Paul Fitzgerald, *Craysea Payslea,* Lynda Kodwyck, *Pirate of the LobStars,* Inger Gregory, *Lobsternardo Da Vinci,* Blythe Brown, *Chix Lobster,* Marsha Zavez, *Picasso Lobster,* Marsha Zavez

Corporate Lobster, Inger Gregory
Effervescent, JoAnn Albano

Lighthouse LobStars Group

Green Lobster, Danielle Ackerman

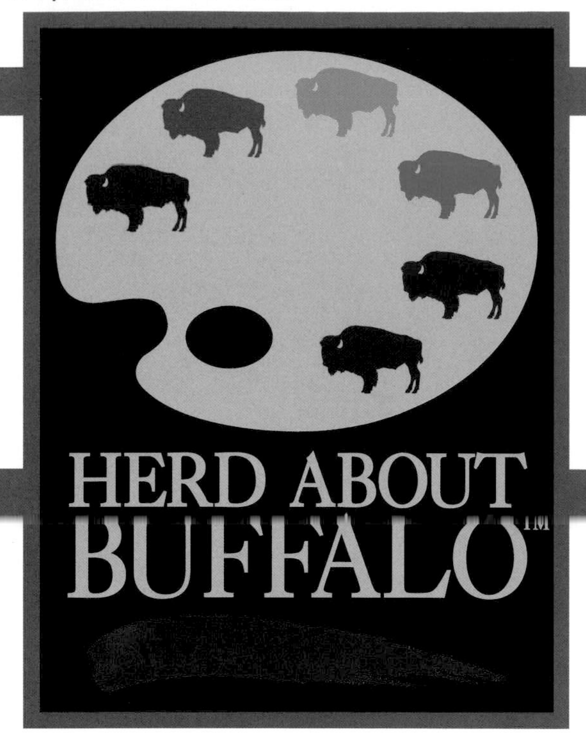

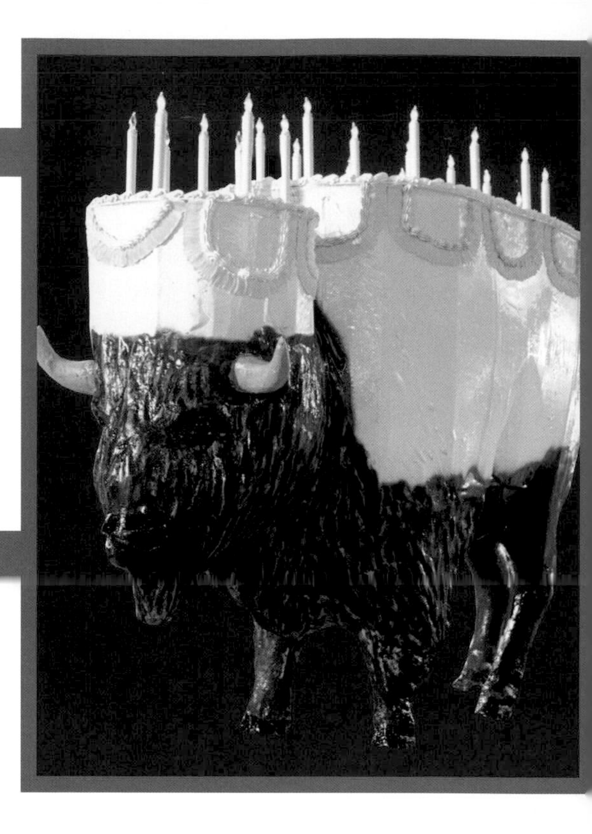

Above: *Buffalo Rocks*, William Davis Wilson
Right: *Buffalo Birthday Cake*, Mark Taylor

Buffalo, New York

"A mid-summer bride was startled to find a well-dressed buffalo among her wedding guests."

Left to right: *Think He'll Make It?*, Craig Palm, *The Head & Tail Buffalo*, Albert Gilewicz, *Buffalo Blooms*, Fotini Renzoni, *Broadway Bison*, Doris M. Collins, Daniel Predmore and Donna White

Above: *FAN-demonium*, Koree Gilbert
Left: *Wind Up/Round Up*, Michael Morgulis

Above: *Reflection*, Natasha Fedor
Right: *Bud the Blooming Buffalo*, Rita Argen Auerbach

Western New Yorkers have been known to celebrate just about anything – the anniversary of a city-debilitating blizzard, obscure holidays, absolutely anything to do with their professional sports teams. The arrival in town of fiberglass animals fashioned to look like big, lumbering buffaloes naturally ignited this party-mania.

Anticipation grew, as sightings of the beasts in the process of being transformed were reported and discussed in offices, cafes and at social gatherings. The buzz built to a crescendo when the buffaloes stampeded into town. Suited up in all the colors of the rainbow, they became honored guests at celebrations of their own unveilings, at barbecues and picnics. A mid-summer bride was startled to find a well-dressed buffalo among her wedding guests.

Herd About Buffalo™ thundered into the hearts of Buffalonians with one hundred fifty-four lifesize buffalo in a summer-long exhibition that changed lives. With the arrival of fall, the herd was rounded-up and auctioned at the Shea's Performing Art Center and over $2 million was raised to support the Roswell Park Cancer Institute in Buffalo, New York.

Above: *Balmy Buffalo*, Wilson Art School Students and Jeffrey Dabill
Right: *Buffalo, a City of Eagle Vision*, Lisa Karwas

DOGNY® New York, New York

America's Tribute to Search and Rescue Dogs

Subway Map Dog
Jolanta Pienczykowski and Stephen Lugo

Heart Of Gold, Kerry Bonner

New York Patriot, C. M. Gross

From early times to the Oklahoma City bombing and the events of September 11, 2001, history has shown that dogs perform an instrumental service to mankind under extraordinary circumstances. *DOGNY*® was the American Kennel Club's way to express appreciation and thanks to the Search and Rescue dogs and their handlers who work hard for our communities and our nation every day of the year.

Conceived as a public art exhibition and fundraiser for Canine Search and Rescue in the event of another catastrophe, *DOGNY*® has raised over $3.2 million to date.

This extraordinary K9 exhibition consisted of over one hundred life-sized sculptures of a German Shepherd painted by artists with a special design for each dog. Many were unveiled at events around New York City. A *DOGNY*® Day was held at Yankee Stadium. A salute to *DOGNY*® took place on the Great White Way and in front of FAO Schwarz. Supermodel Heidi Klum unveiled her very own creation called "Dog With Butterflies" at General Motors Plaza. And the American Kennel Club continues to keep Canine Search and Rescue in the public eye with ongoing *DOGNY*® events.

Iris' Irises, Peter Soriano with Francesca Soriano

Broadway Loves DOGNY, Billy Courage

Courage, Robert L. Braun

"DOGNY® was the American Kennel Club's way to express appreciation and thanks to the Search and Rescue dogs and their handlers..."

Wall Street Dog
Jolanta Pienczykowski and Stephen Lugo

K-9 Ladder
Paul Farinacci

Pride
Dean Johnson

Setting the Pace
Mike Neville

Chairs on Parade

Charlotte, North Carolina

Cardinal Chair
Maria Wiatrowski

Virtually Infinite
Jimmy O'Neal

Cycladic Chair
Andrew Coats

Chair Descending the Staircase
Northwest School of the Arts
Visual Arts Department

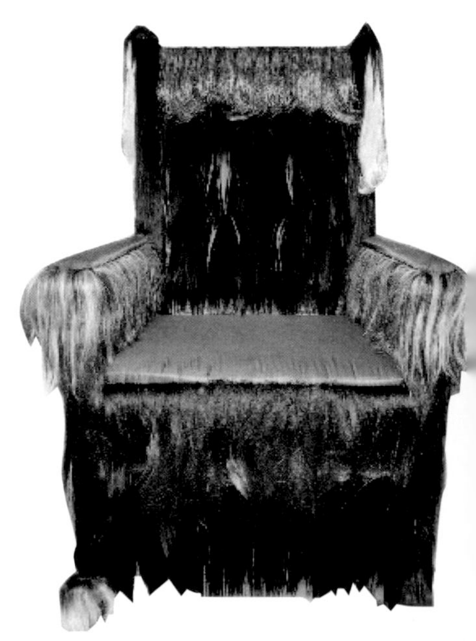

Hair Chair
Kim Alsbrooks

Fractured View
Independence High School
Visual Arts Department

Rocking chairs are for rocking, right? In most places this would be true. However, in Charlotte, North Carolina over one hundred chairs rocked like they never had before. Some chairs were converted into people, celebrities and caricatures. There were chairs on roller skates and chairs turned into pieces of urban architecture. Other than the fact that they all began as chairs, the only other thing they had in common was each took on a life and personality of its own.

The furniture industry and the low-country rocking chair design are part of North Carolina's regional heritage. Indeed, the state is renowned as the leader for furniture design and production in the United States. So it was a matter of blending history with the talents of contemporary artists from around North and South Carolina, that brought this icon to the shops, restaurants, office buildings and parks of Charlotte.

The Tyron Center for Visual Art sponsored *Chairs on Parade* and was the beneficiary of a portion of the proceeds, along with many other national non-profit organizations.

"Other than the fact that they all began as chairs, the only thing they had in common was each took on a life and personality of its own."

Womanist
Lena Hopkins-Jackson

Net Chair
John S. Morrison

North Carolina Beach Chair
Martha Matthews

UnFORKettable

Greater Grand Forks is a bustling community surrounded by a mosaic of Upper Midwest farm country. Native American tribes settled here, followed by trappers and traders who set up a trading post where two major rivers converged. Early farming settlers followed, and a town took shape that grew into a city with the introduction of the railroad into the region.

This lively, artistic city is filled with rich traditions. Festivals are a part of its storied history. "Winnipeg Day," an international "Crazy Days" conceived in 1900, was designed to attract Canadians to the city. "First Night" is a New Years celebration that brings people from miles around to stroll downtown, check out the entertainment, and admire the ice sculptures.

A similar spirit accounted for the community's decision to mount *UnFORKettable Art* – which featured not your usual cutlery, but fancifully painted and embellished 6-foot forks installed in various outdoor locations throughout the city, many of which remain on display today. Residents and visitors were left with some warm memories from this exhibition in the Grand Cities.

UnFORKettable Art was the perfect collaboration between the arts, businesses and two non-profit agencies that benefited from the sale of these works of art: Healthy Families Region IV and the Community Violence Intervention Center.

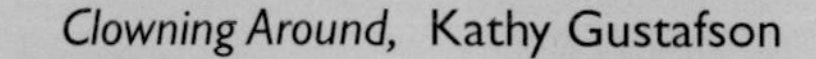

Clowning Around, Kathy Gustafson

Grand Forks Depot, Kim Dohrman

Floral Fantasia, Eunice Kuhn

ART

Grand Forks and East Grand Forks, North Dakota

not your usual cutlery

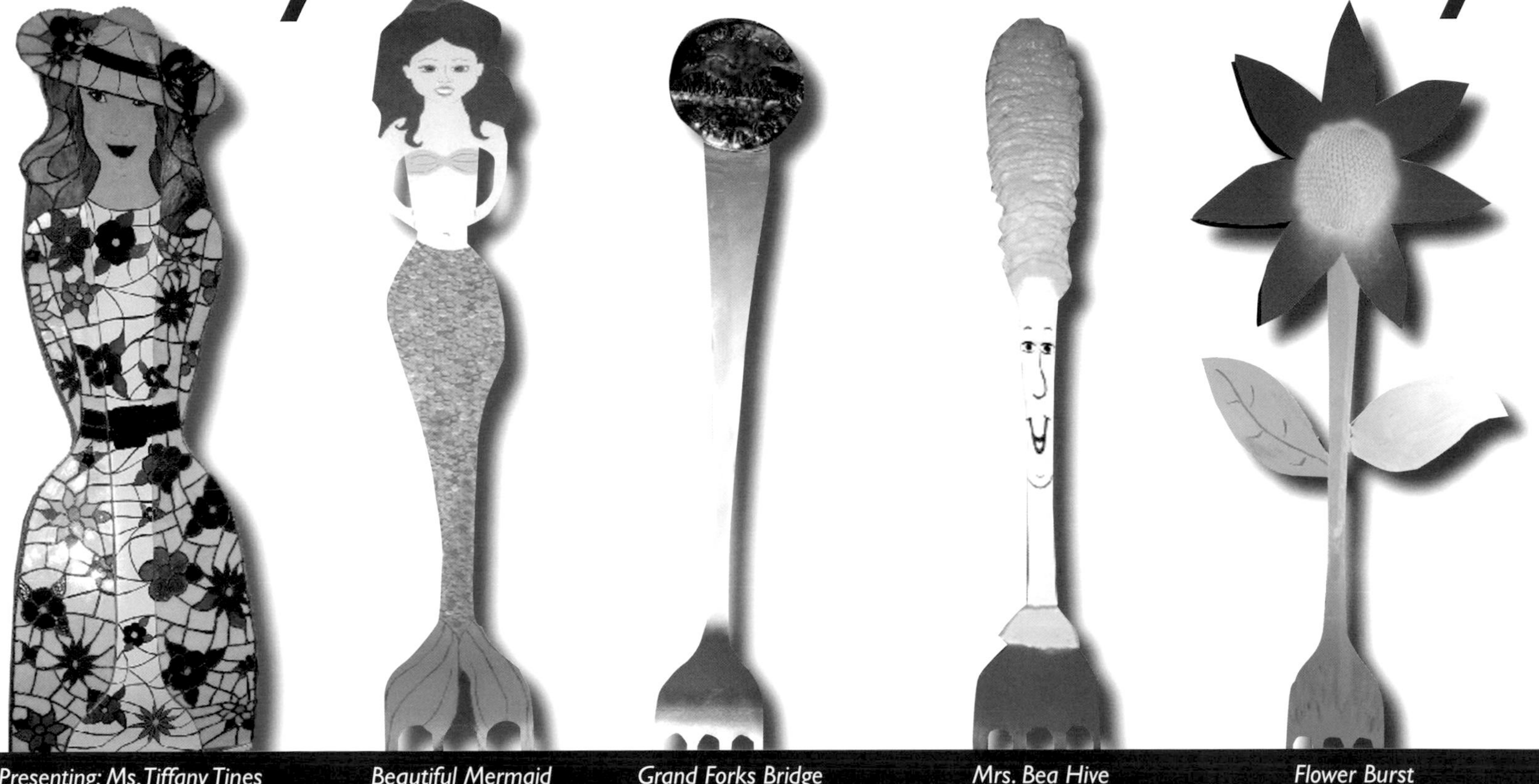

Presenting: Ms. Tiffany Tines
Tana Rangel

Beautiful Mermaid
Meghan Boushee

Grand Forks Bridge
Kim Dohrman

Mrs. Bea Hive
Rosemary Gasal

Flower Burst
Meghan Boushee

"Not your usual cutlery, *UnFORKettable Art* featured fancifully painted and embellished 6-foot forks."

THE BIG PIG GIG™

Cincinnati, Ohio

Swine Lake
T.A. Boyle

ART works

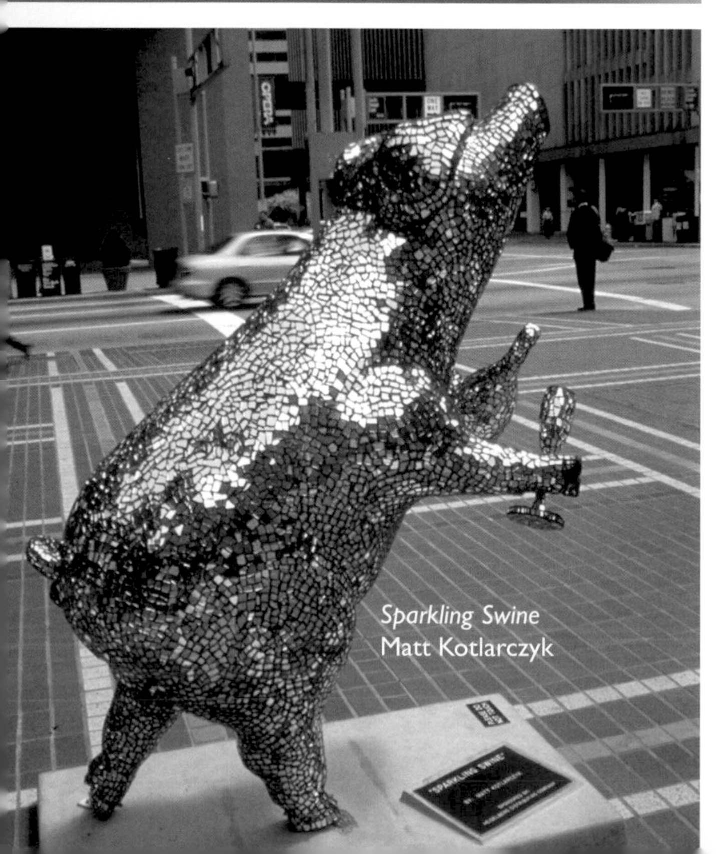

Sparkling Swine
Matt Kotlarczyk

Cincinnati was transformed into "Cin-sow-nati" when decorated fiberglass pig sculptures - sitting, standing, walking, with or without wings - overran the city. Artists went "hog wild" with their designs. Many pigs donned hats, shoes, eyelashes, wheels and other elaborate additions. Well-known characters made appearances in pig art: "Michael-ham-gelo," "Pig-asso," "Ernest Ham-mingway," "Ham-let" and "Pork-eman," to name a few. People "squealed with delight" and took thousands of "pig-tures" as they walked around looking at the pigs, each more creative than the last. Pigs were the summer-long "media hogs." There was nothing "boar-ing" about the event. It was the world's largest "pig-nic."

And so it went, with people alternately groaning and smiling at the pigs and puns of the *The Big Pig Gig*™.

Produced by ArtWorks, an award-winning arts-based employment and job training program for youth in the greater Cincinnati region, *The Big Pig Gig*™ was about Cincinnatians having fun with their shared "porkopolis history" while raising close to $1 million for over two hundred local non-profit organizations.

Uncle Ham
Heather Chitwood

Pigasus
Lynn Judd

Styler Davidson Sow-tain
Lynne, Scott and Steve Hamons

"Well-known characters made appearances in pig art: 'Michael-ham-gelo,' 'Pig-asso,' 'Ham-let' and 'Pork-emon,' to name a few."

Topigary
Leslie Shiels

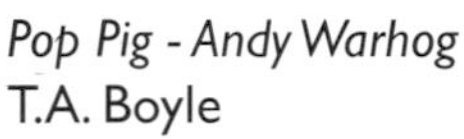

Pop Pig - Andy Warhog
T.A. Boyle

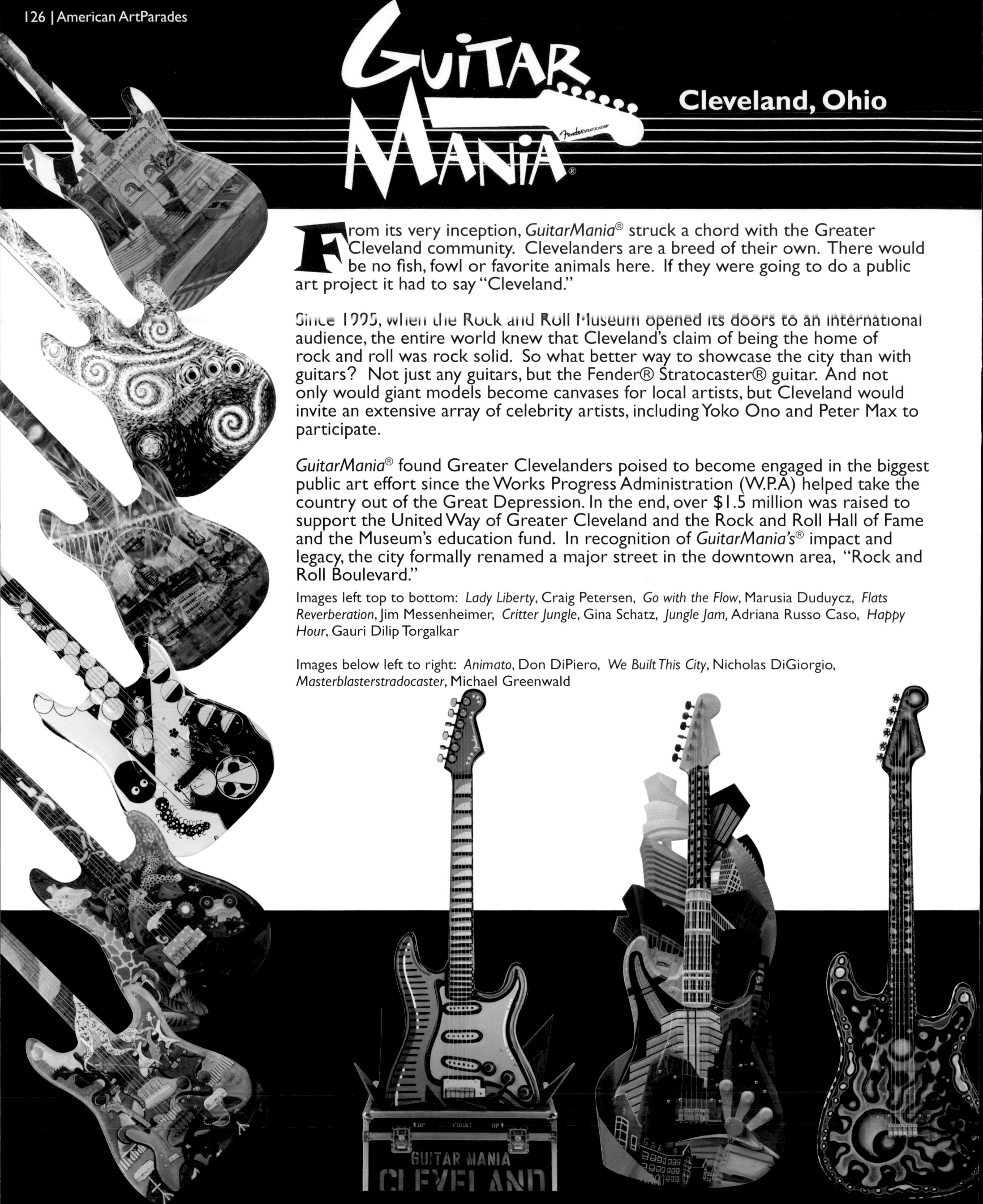

GuitarMania® Cleveland, Ohio

From its very inception, *GuitarMania*® struck a chord with the Greater Cleveland community. Clevelanders are a breed of their own. There would be no fish, fowl or favorite animals here. If they were going to do a public art project it had to say "Cleveland."

Since 1995, when the Rock and Roll Museum opened its doors to an international audience, the entire world knew that Cleveland's claim of being the home of rock and roll was rock solid. So what better way to showcase the city than with guitars? Not just any guitars, but the Fender® Stratocaster® guitar. And not only would giant models become canvases for local artists, but Cleveland would invite an extensive array of celebrity artists, including Yoko Ono and Peter Max to participate.

GuitarMania® found Greater Clevelanders poised to become engaged in the biggest public art effort since the Works Progress Administration (W.P.A) helped take the country out of the Great Depression. In the end, over $1.5 million was raised to support the United Way of Greater Cleveland and the Rock and Roll Hall of Fame and the Museum's education fund. In recognition of *GuitarMania's*® impact and legacy, the city formally renamed a major street in the downtown area, "Rock and Roll Boulevard."

Images left top to bottom: *Lady Liberty*, Craig Petersen, *Go with the Flow*, Marusia Duduycz, *Flats Reverberation*, Jim Messenheimer, *Critter Jungle*, Gina Schatz, *Jungle Jam,* Adriana Russo Caso, *Happy Hour*, Gauri Dilip Torgalkar

Images below left to right: *Animato*, Don DiPiero, *We Built This City*, Nicholas DiGiorgio, *Masterblasterstradocaster*, Michael Greenwald

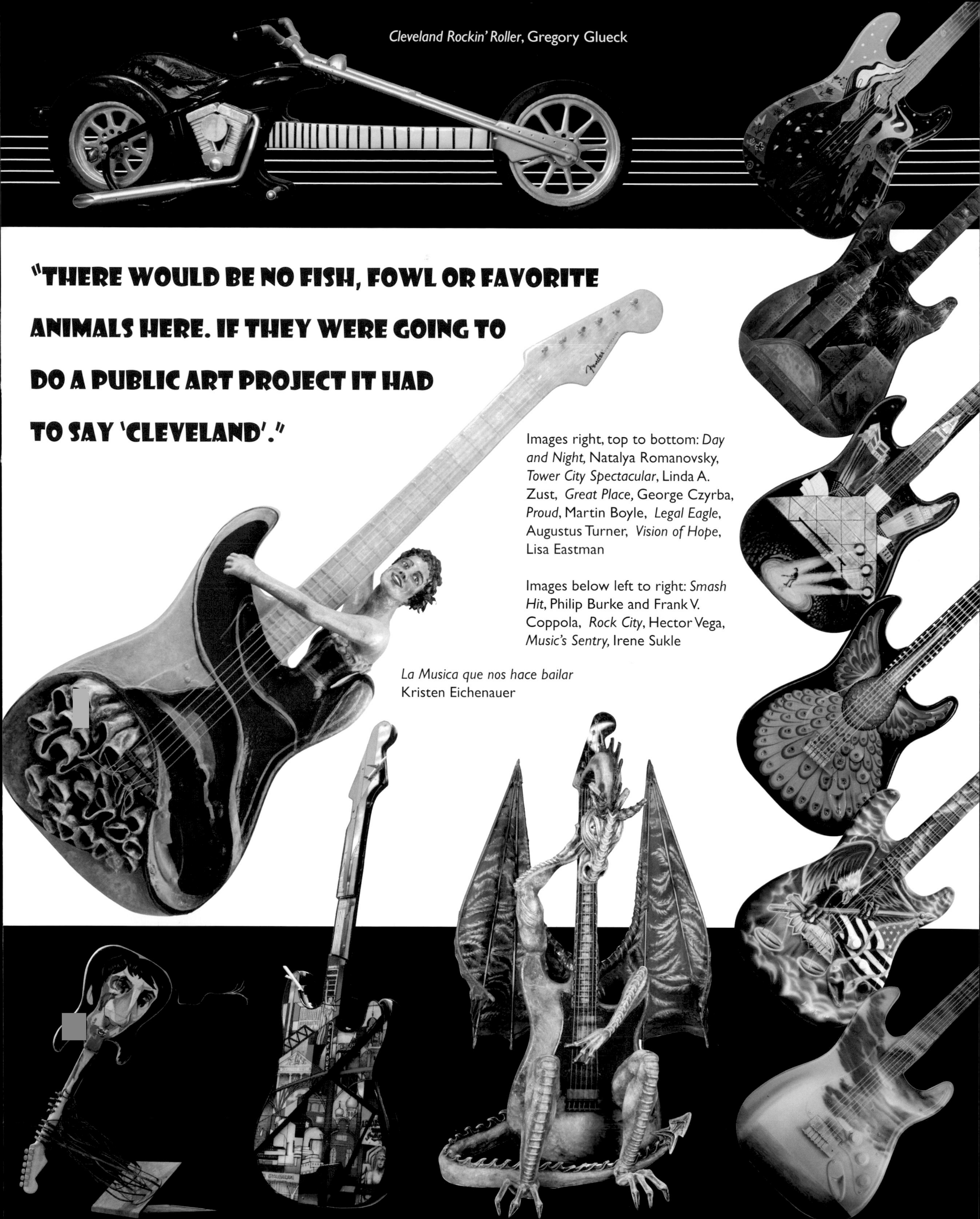

Cleveland Rockin' Roller, Gregory Glueck

"THERE WOULD BE NO FISH, FOWL OR FAVORITE ANIMALS HERE. IF THEY WERE GOING TO DO A PUBLIC ART PROJECT IT HAD TO SAY 'CLEVELAND'."

Images right, top to bottom: *Day and Night,* Natalya Romanovsky, *Tower City Spectacular*, Linda A. Zust, *Great Place,* George Czyrba, *Proud*, Martin Boyle, *Legal Eagle*, Augustus Turner, *Vision of Hope*, Lisa Eastman

Images below left to right: *Smash Hit*, Philip Burke and Frank V. Coppola, *Rock City*, Hector Vega, *Music's Sentry,* Irene Sukle

La Musica que nos hace bailar
Kristen Eichenauer

SPIRIT OF THE BUFFALO

Oklahoma City, Oklahoma

"Artists bring to life these magnificent ambassadors to protect the last great places in Oklahoma."

Oklahoma's Pride
Babetta Juergens
and Doug Swindell

From left: *Pride*, John A. Perkins, *Dream Spirits*, Kathryn L. Bailey

If it were a movie its title would be, "The Return of the Buffalo." But it was a public art project conceived as a way of raising awareness and funds for the Oklahoma Chapter of The Nature Conservancy, whose mission is to protect the natural landscapes and streams in Oklahoma.

One hundred of the state's most talented artists were invited to work their artistic magic on the state animal. Not to be confused with the hardy and robust species which has roamed the range for more than 5,000 years, the aim of this "herd" was to delight and entertain. Which it did. One top of the Van Gogh buffalo's horn was missing. Another buffalo wore roller skates, dispelling the notion that you can't roller-skate in a buffalo herd.

Residents and visitors held "buffalo hunts" – touring Oklahoma City on bikes, by car or on foot – to see the unique details of each buffalo up close. Judging from the overwhelming popularity, the artfully painted buffaloes were the perfect "nature" ambassadors to carry the message that the last great wild places in Oklahoma need to be protected before they are gone.

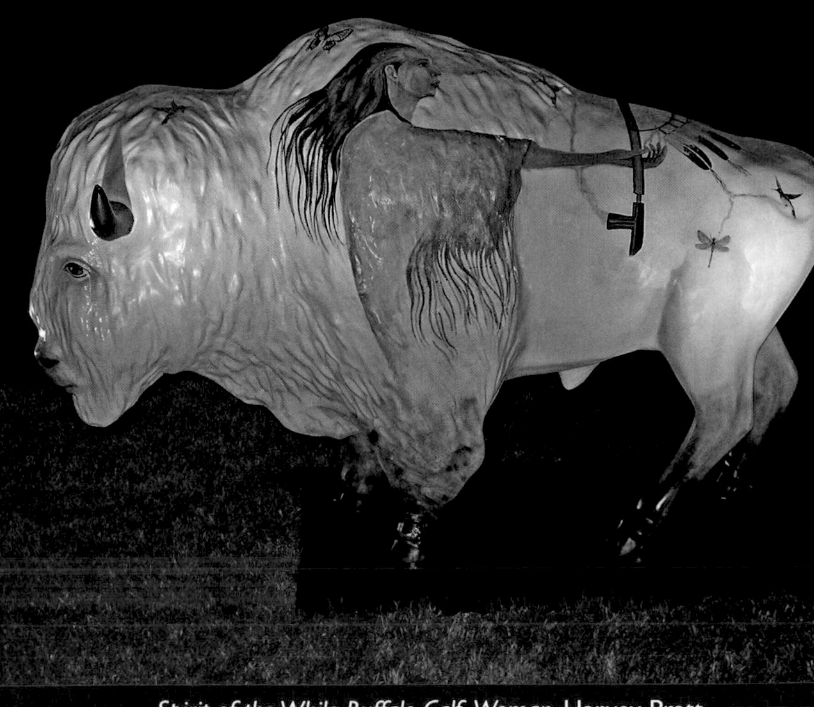

Spirit of the While Buffalo Calf Woman, Harvey Pratt

Blue Suede Hooves
Julie Wells

Buffalo Nickel
Rick Bewley

Zubee the Zuffalo
Brantley Cowan

Jules II
Dale Chihuly

Blooming Buddy Bison, Pamela R. Kirkham

Oaxacan Buffalo, Tracey Bewley

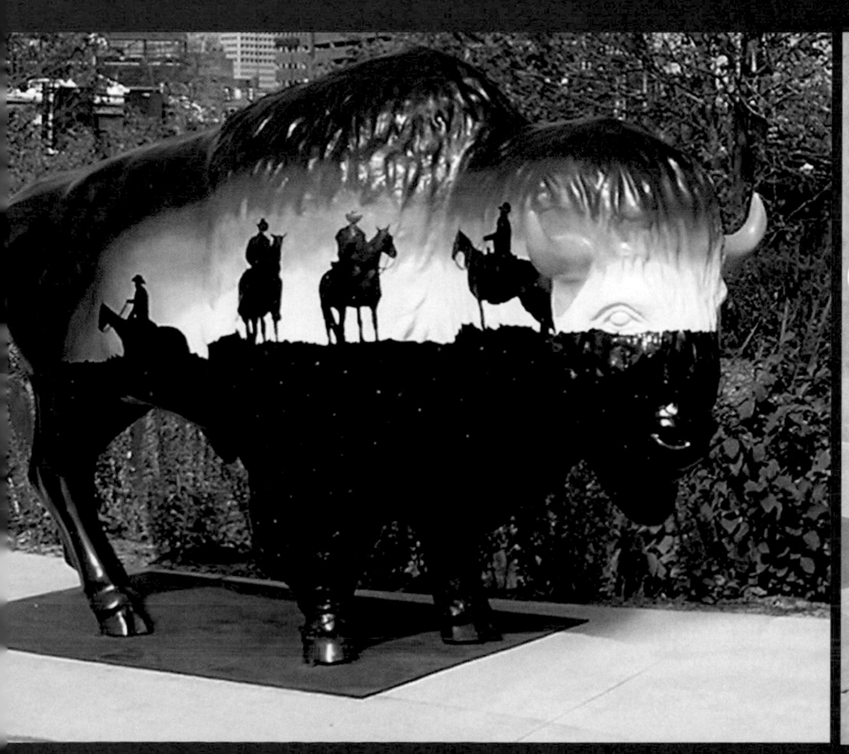

Made of Cowboy Stars, Jason Clay Lewis

Buffalo Bench, Adrienne Day, Todd Davenport, Don West and Western Village Academy Children

DUCKS ON PARADE

Eugene, Oregon

Lively and colorful. Funny and playful. Whimsical and wild. Six-foot tall, artistic Big Ducks flocked to downtown Eugene all summer long. The following year, the Big Ducks returned for a reunion tour. The entire community got quacky, shaking out its tail feathers for a Big Duck Walk-a-Thon that toured various nesting sites, turning Eugene into a veritable pleasure park.

"You were the wind beneath our wings," said the organizers to the businesses, organizations and artists who helped the project take flight. The fun culminated with a live auction that was such a quacking success, a new flock flew into town the following summer. *Ducks on Parade* provided a very unique fundraising mechanism for Lane County Charities, Lane County Schools and The Downtown Initiative for the Visual Arts, which helped to strengthen and revitalize downtown Eugene as a regional arts and entertainment center.

Buckarette Duck
Christine Pendergrass

Big Ducks stand as sentries for the Big Duck Reunion

Fleur de Duck
Donna Briggs

"You were the wind beneath our wings."

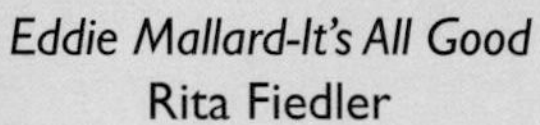

Eddie Mallard-It's All Good
Rita Fiedler

Images left, top to bottom: *Ducks on Parade,* Jani Hoberg, *On the Fly,* Kandi and Kevin White, *Earth Duck,* Michael Alferes, *Handy Dandy Duck,* Donna Briggs and KidJam Kids, *Delilah the Duck Call Girl*, Susan Selig

Images right, top to bottom: *Closet Duck Fan,* Rita Fiedler, *Meduckal Rescue,* Donna Briggs, *Fertile Myrtle*, Shari Hulse, *One Bright Duck*, Jay and Julie Moore and Mike Backus. *Crazy Quilt Quacker,* LaVonne Tarbox-Crone

Natures Child
Linda Killion Smith

Grants Pass "Bearfest"

Grants Pass, Oregon

Tesseroe
Christine Gagnon

Pharooh Bear
Alan Lauire

Cub Tut
Alan Lauire

Cub in a Tub
Mark Willis

Beary Serenade
Janet Higgins

Afternoon of a Bear
Mark and Kay Fontaine

Huckle Berry
Michael Murphy

Chocolate Covered Samurai Bear
Travis Gagnon

Bloomin Bear
Vicki Magallon

Wilbear
E. B. Effects and Design Co.

Applegate the Cub-A-Neer
Julie Bickle

Classical Cub
Janet HIggins

Pierre Bear the Arteest and La Petite Monique, Del and Veronica Hearn

Bears are wild animals that prefer wild places and avoid human contact. But one summer in Grant's Pass, Oregon they overcame their shyness and joined with locals in an event intended to attract tourists to the Rogue River area and "give paws" to visitors. What happened was called *Grants Pass "Bearfest,"* but it could just as easily have been referred to as "Bears Gone Wild." Artfully interpreted in every imaginable way, the bedecked, bejeweled and bodacious bruins took over the town, adding a new chapter to the rich history and vibrant culture of this Southern Oregon community. "No one could have predicted how popular the bears would be," said Brady Adams, President and CEO of Evergreen Federal Bank and orignator of *"Bearfest."* Local non-profit organizations and artists benefited from the wildly succcessful auction of these "Wild Bears."

Tourist Bear
Linda Killion Smith

Bear the Spirit, Share the Story & Indian Mary
Mary Durham

"Artfullly interpreted in every imaginable way, the bedecked, bejeweled and bodacious bruins took over town."

SALMON IN THE CITY

Salem, Oregon

Sustainable Keys- Fairview Unlocked
Alan and Mary Lou Zeek

Technicolor Coho Buck
Jim Mattingly

Zula, Queen of Zambezi
Marcus Linter

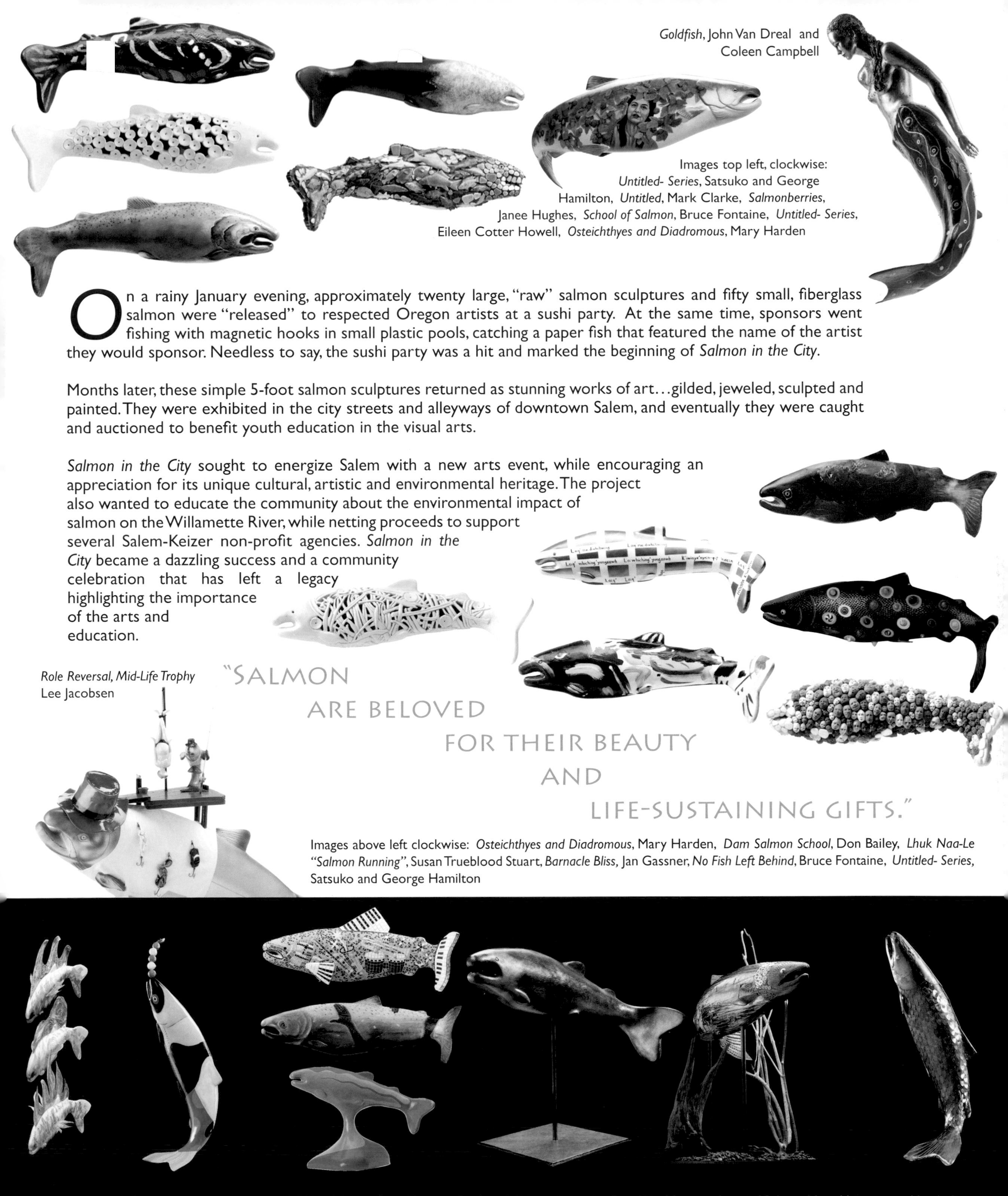

Goldfish, John Van Dreal and Coleen Campbell

Images top left, clockwise: *Untitled- Series*, Satsuko and George Hamilton, *Untitled*, Mark Clarke, *Salmonberries*, Janee Hughes, *School of Salmon*, Bruce Fontaine, *Untitled- Series*, Eileen Cotter Howell, *Osteichthyes and Diadromous*, Mary Harden

On a rainy January evening, approximately twenty large, "raw" salmon sculptures and fifty small, fiberglass salmon were "released" to respected Oregon artists at a sushi party. At the same time, sponsors went fishing with magnetic hooks in small plastic pools, catching a paper fish that featured the name of the artist they would sponsor. Needless to say, the sushi party was a hit and marked the beginning of *Salmon in the City*.

Months later, these simple 5-foot salmon sculptures returned as stunning works of art…gilded, jeweled, sculpted and painted. They were exhibited in the city streets and alleyways of downtown Salem, and eventually they were caught and auctioned to benefit youth education in the visual arts.

Salmon in the City sought to energize Salem with a new arts event, while encouraging an appreciation for its unique cultural, artistic and environmental heritage. The project also wanted to educate the community about the environmental impact of salmon on the Willamette River, while netting proceeds to support several Salem-Keizer non-profit agencies. *Salmon in the City* became a dazzling success and a community celebration that has left a legacy highlighting the importance of the arts and education.

Role Reversal, Mid-Life Trophy
Lee Jacobsen

"SALMON ARE BELOVED FOR THEIR BEAUTY AND LIFE-SUSTAINING GIFTS."

Images above left clockwise: *Osteichthyes and Diadromous*, Mary Harden, *Dam Salmon School*, Don Bailey, *Lhuk Naa-Le "Salmon Running"*, Susan Trueblood Stuart, *Barnacle Bliss*, Jan Gassner, *No Fish Left Behind*, Bruce Fontaine, *Untitled- Series*, Satsuko and George Hamilton

Images above left to right, top to bottom: *Fish, Wind & Fire*, Anne Kresge, *Patchwork Salmon Balancing Fruit*, Kim Murton, *Jammin' Salmon*, Mary Heintzman, *Hands On The Salmon*, Kristen Kuhns, *Untitled*, Jim Shull, *Untitled*, Mark Clarke, *Copper River Salmon*, Sara Swanberg, *Copper Skillet*, Joshua McMurrin

GoFish!©

Erie, Pennsylvania

Gumbo, Fishtank Creative

Elfish Presley
Bill Figurski

"Hey, how about we put giant fish all over downtown Erie?"

Wang Chung-Waterworld
Ron Bayuzick

Recycle for the Halibut
D.W. Martin

Charlie, in honor of Charlie Scalise
Abigail Brace

Erie Perch
Carole Werder

"We're hooked on *GoFish!*©... We're up to the gills in fish...This project is fin-tastic... Things are coming along swimmingly... We've been lured by all the colorful creatures..." That's the way people in Erie talked throughout the summer, as fish sculptures were released throughout the city...and, at the end of the project, auctioned off at a Fish Market.

The results happily exceeded the vision of the organizers, and in the afterglow of the exhilaration, in the wake of all the wonderful memories, a new idea for another project was born - *LeapFrog!* would be the next artistic aquatic adventure. Proceeds of *GoFish!*© benefited Gannon University's Scholarship Fund and the Erie Public Art Fund of The Erie Art Museum.

Fish Kiss
Cynthia M. Christopher

Juicy Sushi
Brad Lethaby

Fishkabibble
Susan Moore

Night Swimming
Shelle Barron

Ziegfeld Flounder
Richard Davis

Red Haring
Peggy Brace and Ed Roskowski

Erie, Pennsylvania

Harry Pond-er
Greg Mitchell

Jumping Jester
Steve Stauber, Dave Vitale, Mike Hilbert,

Croakerfeld-Master Illusionist
Kevin R. Irvin,

Several years later, on a warm, summer morning, a crowd of hundreds gathered on the steps of the Erie Art Museum. They were armed with cameras and poised with cell phones, and all eyes were focused on an oversized egg that had appeared during the night. Shortly after the clock struck nine the egg was cracked, revealing a... sitting frog. A cheer arose from all around as *LeapFrog!* was launched. Proceeds of *LeapFrog!* benefited Gannon University's Scholarship Fund and the Erie Art Museum.

"At a time when so much that happens in the world divides us, the frogs have brought people together."

Images above, left to right: *Welcome to Frogeritaville*, Jesse and Morgan Brace, *Toadilly Elvis*, Chuck Dill, *Herk Tuxberry*, Timothy W. Blair
Images below, left to right, top to bottom: *Helo-Hopper*, Bob and Scott Smith, *Colorfully Close*, Fort LeBoeuf Advanced Art Students, *Jazzy Frog In The Moon*, Susan Moore and Gary Schneider, *Amphibious Acoustician*, Joseph Allen Popp, *Frog Shui*, Luke Gehring, *One Frog Band*, Tom Hubert

Blackstone River Valley
New England's Historic National Park Area

Samuel Slater Mill Racer, Paul Gordon and Chris Nichols

Blackstone Valley

The Story of a Farm, Laura O. Cenedella

Southwick's Zoo Canoe, Elinor Murray

Preserve Massachusetts Wildlife, Kristin Morrill

America Runs on Dunkin, Chris Nichols

"The program was designed to attract people to the Blackstone Valley through the display of 15-foot long canoes decorated by local artists."

Canoe Trail

Pawtucket, Rhode Island

In a creative departure from the traditional, animal-themed outdoor public art projects, a Rhode Island tourism collaborative based in the Blackstone River Valley, one of New England's historic national park areas, decided to undertake something uniquely its own.

Called *The Blackstone Canoe Trail*, the program was designed to attract people to the Blackstone River Valley through the display of 15-foot long canoes decorated by local artists and "beached" around town. Visitors and residents, together with their families and friends, were then challenged to discover these canoes throughout the Blackstone Valley, have a personal photo taken with each canoe found, and then submit their photos by e-mail to the program's website. The entrant photographed with the most canoes would be eligible to win a 15-foot fiberglass canoe, with paddles and life jackets for four.

Images left top to bottom: *New England's Historic Playground,* Chris Nichols, *The S.S. Cricket,* Chris Nichols, *Koopman's Canoe,* Chris Nichols

The Blackstone Blue Canoe, Chris Nichols

CAROUSEL HORSES ON PARADE

Myrtle Beach, South Carolina

Officer Joe, Dixie Dugan

Dragonfly Dancer, Sherry W. Kelley

PaPa's Pepper, Patrick Todd and Family

Mare-Y Christmas, Ruth Cox

Beaded Beauty, Jo Anne Doshier

The golden age of carousels, when craftsmen chiseled, painted, and delivered a special breed of American horse to an adoring public, lasted only two decades - from 1905 to 1925. The crash of 1929 forced many carousel manufacturers out of business. Today carousels still exist but there are precious few. One superb survivor is the historic carousel that has been operating at the Pavilion Amusement Park in Myrtle Beach, South Carolina for more than 50 years.

Below left to right: *Mare-E-Go-Round*, Kay Payne, *GaShmare*, Ed Fanjoy, *Fund Racer*, Marilyn Hester, *Gotcha Covered*, Jackie Stacharowski

"INSTEAD OF PRANCING IN A CIRCLE TO CALLIOPE MUSIC, THESE FROLICSOME, BRIGHTLY DECORATED CAROUSEL HORSES ROAMED FREELY AROUND TOWN."

Shell-Sea the Seahorse, Jenny Lane *Liberty and Justice For All,* Linda B. Weatherspoon *Palmetto Pride*, Jamie Sharpe

'oomers, Sudie Payne Daves *Monarch*, Javier Vega, Jr. *Mare de la Mer*, Cate Ferreira and Amy Simon *Beacon Blues*, Mary Douglass

Visitors and residents in Myrtle Beach were treated to a revival of sorts... only this time, instead of prancing in a circle to calliope music, these frolicsome, brightly decorated carousel horses roamed freely around town. In the fall they were gathered and auctioned to raise money for the renovation of the Rivoli Theater, the local vintage movie house. The Peoples' Choice winner, "Mare-E-Go-Round," was held out of the auction to be permanently displayed in the lobby of this historic theater.

Below left to right: *Sea Biscuit*, Diana J. Canaday, *Chicora Chic*, Esther S. Hellaby, *Origami Express*, Jefri and Rick Chandler and Margo Mohan, *Carolina Comfort*, Nancy Bracken

CUSTER STAMPEDE

Custer, South Dakota

"A GENTLER KIND OF BISON NOW STAMPEDES WITH THE WILD BUFFALO IN CUSTER STATE PARK."

Kathy Morrow and Chief David Bald Eagle

Blackbirds Watching, Dennis Cumin

The Journey, Steven Fink

Joe, Nikki Sigle

Sacred Stars, Pati Deuter

Each autumn, thousands of spectators come to see the bison stampede across Custer State Park during the annual Buffalo Roundup, held just a few miles from the city of Custer. It's here that one of the largest publicly-owned herds of bison wanders freely across the grasslands, proving that the West is still pretty wild, a place where buffalo do indeed roam.

A gentler kind of bison now stampedes with the wild buffalo in Custer State Park. Christened the *Custer Stampede*, this annual cultural event features dozens of decorated bison displayed on the street corners of Custer. The bison are also at locations around the Black Hills throughout the summer months, conjuring images of the Western frontier and American Indian life, while at the same time showcasing the visions of regional artists.

The *Custer Stampede* is an annual cultural event and a partnership between the Custer Area Chamber of Commerce and the Custer Area Arts Council, designed to help fund future arts and economic development projects.

Images right, top to bottom: *Sacred Stars,* Pati Deuter, *The Spirit Within Us*, Paula Tonemah

American Bull, Dwayne Wilcox

Times Change, Sonja Huff

Nashville's GuitarTown

Nashville, Tennessee

What better symbol of Nashville and country music than the guitar? What more clever use of the guitar than to invite visual artists to paint ten-foot tall Gibson Guitar sculptures in eye-catching ways that show off the heritage and spirit of Music City?

Presented by Gibson Guitar, the idea was given a visual life of its own by local visual artists, many of whom collaborated with such country music greats as Dolly Parton, Charlie Daniels, Wynonna, Diamond Rio, and Sara Evans. With each guitar, a different and inspiring aspect of Nashville was portrayed. With visitors and residents alike, *Nashville's GuitarTown* struck a chord. These spectacular guitars were auctioned off with the proceeds benefiting the Country Music Hall of Fame and Museum, Nashville's United Way, The DISTRICT, and the Cystic Fibrosis Foundation. Look for GuitarTown in Austin, London and other cities in the future.

God Bless Texas
Jason Sorey

Heartbreak Hotel
Alan Rhody

Flutter
Katherine Falk

Wizard of Waukesha
Trey Eckles

Road to the Opry
Bryan C. Adams

Let Freedom Sing
Paige Easter and
Dan Goostree

Twang!
Doug Jones

Music of a Woman
Claire Burns

Keeping It Real In Nashville
Michael Cooper

Country Sunset
Katie Roller Schulz

Roy Orbison
Rob Hendon

Chet Atkin's Southern Gentleman
Jim Sherraden

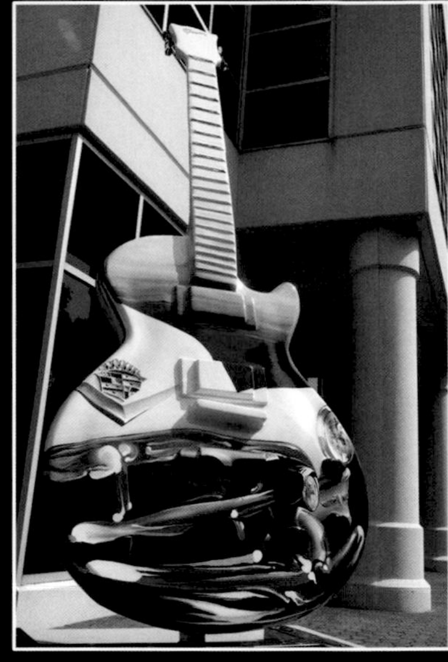

Lost & Lonesome
Brian Tull

Nashville The Beautiful
Juliana Ericson

The Driving Force
In Entertainment
Barbara Coon and Brad Gaidos

Spiritual Music
Barbara Gronefeld

Manuel Original
Manuel

Orange Blossom Special
Marsha Rusk

Live Music
Rachel Kice

Van Zandt
Will Van Zandt

They Started It
Sheila Bartlett

Dallas Soars!

Dallas, Texas

No single icon is more appropriate to carry the message of Dallas than the mighty Pegasus.

It all goes back to the 1930s, when an enormous, rotating Pegasus was installed on top of the tallest building in downtown Dallas. The "flying red horse" of Mobil Oil fame was a symbol that Dallas had arrived - as a dynamic city, and as a center for petroleum. In fact, there were two horses, back to back, and they could be seen for 75 miles in any direction. Some said this was done just so no one could ever say Dallas was a "one-horse town." In reality, it signified much more than that. It stated to the world that the "Old West" wasn't old anymore.

It was therefore natural that Pegasus sculptures would be selected to represent Dallas in the artistic festival *Dallas Soars!* One hundred eighty-five unique flying horses were displayed throughout downtown Dallas. Eventually thirty of the sponsors donated their horses for an auction with proceeds benefiting Arts Partners and Adopt-A-Monument, two local non-profit arts organizations.

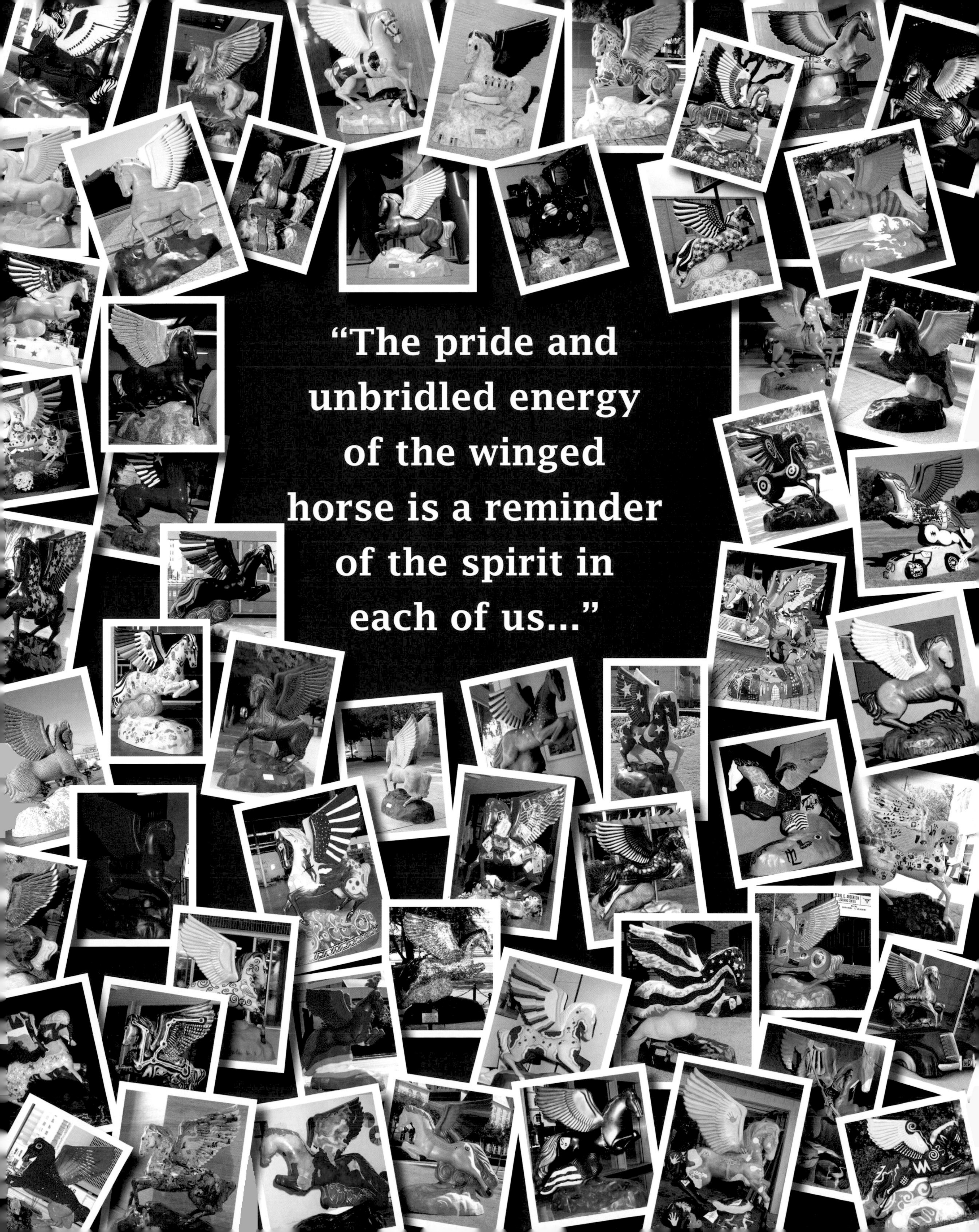
"The pride and
unbridled energy
of the winged
horse is a reminder
of the spirit in
each of us..."

Regale Yourself With Flowers, Brilliant Like The Sun
Susan Davidoff

"What is it that symbolizes El Paso?" they asked. The answer: "The sun!"

Art and Sol

El Paso, Texas

Garden Sun, David Nakabayashi

El Ojo Del Sol – Eye of the Sun
El Paso Independent School District and Chapin High School Students

El Paso Under The Sun, Lyuba Titovets

Corona Del Sol – Crown of Sun
Cesar Ivan

Aguila O Sol – Flip of the Coin
Francisco Enrique Delgado

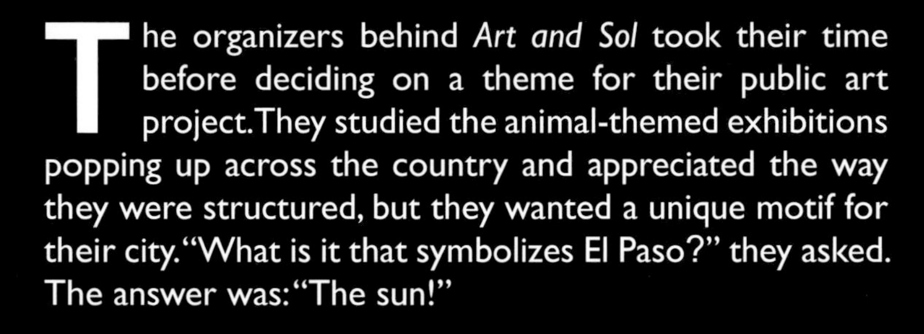

The organizers behind *Art and Sol* took their time before deciding on a theme for their public art project. They studied the animal-themed exhibitions popping up across the country and appreciated the way they were structured, but they wanted a unique motif for their city. "What is it that symbolizes El Paso?" they asked. The answer was: "The sun!"

So they came up with a proclamation that read, in part:

"Whereas the sun's importance to all forms of life remains paramount

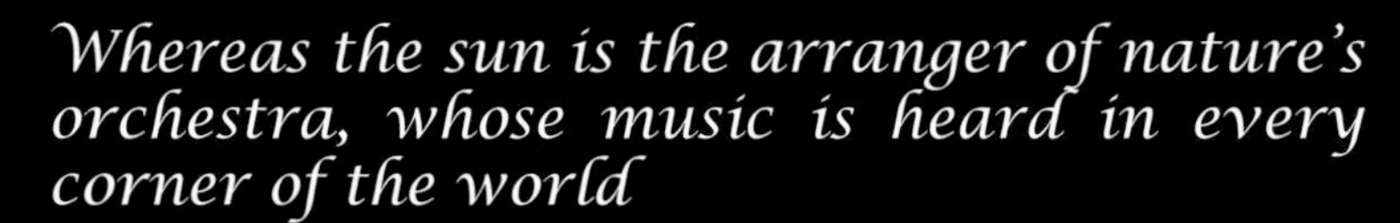

Whereas the sun is the arranger of nature's orchestra, whose music is heard in every corner of the world

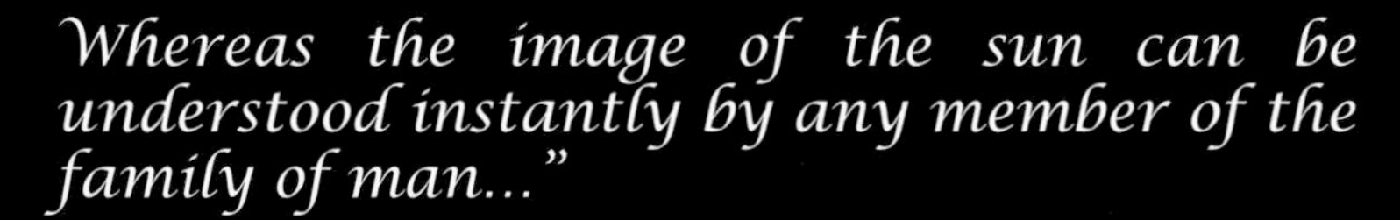

Whereas the image of the sun can be understood instantly by any member of the family of man..."

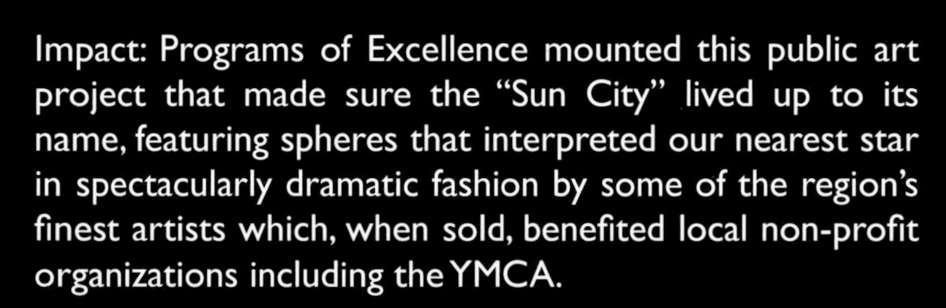

Impact: Programs of Excellence mounted this public art project that made sure the "Sun City" lived up to its name, featuring spheres that interpreted our nearest star in spectacularly dramatic fashion by some of the region's finest artists which, when sold, benefited local non-profit organizations including the YMCA.

Prometheus, Mora

Seasons of the Sun, Carlos Callejo

The Shining Desert Suns – Giver and Taker of Life, Susan Klahr

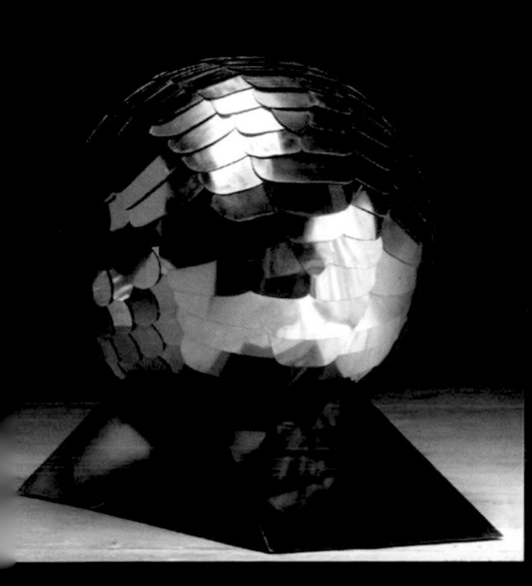

Armored Sol, Willie Ray Parish

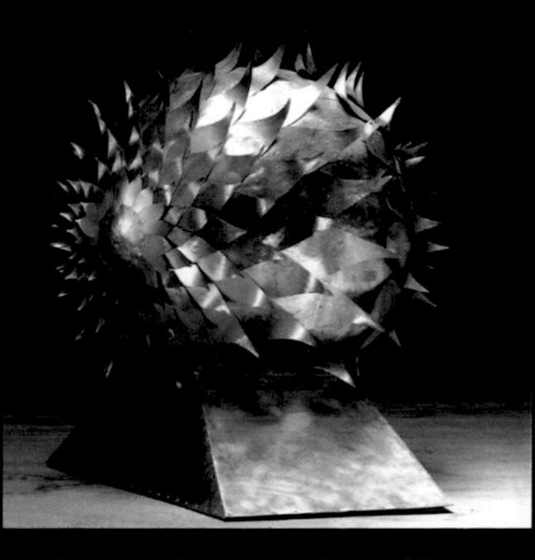

Sun and Sol, Aaron Royal Mosley

From the Sol, Geronimo Garcia

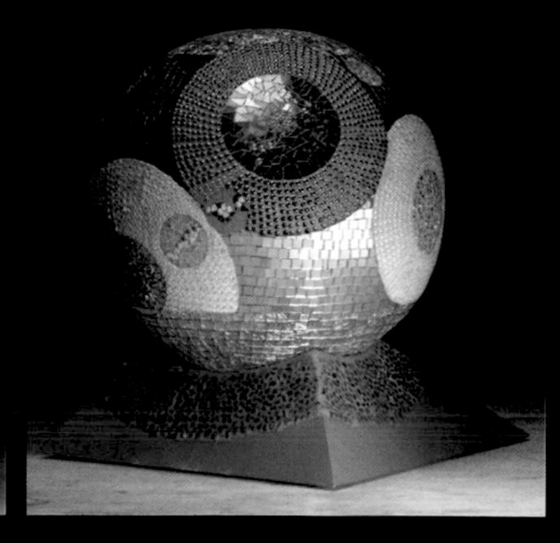

Sunspots – The Sun of All Parts
Meralee Schlusselberg

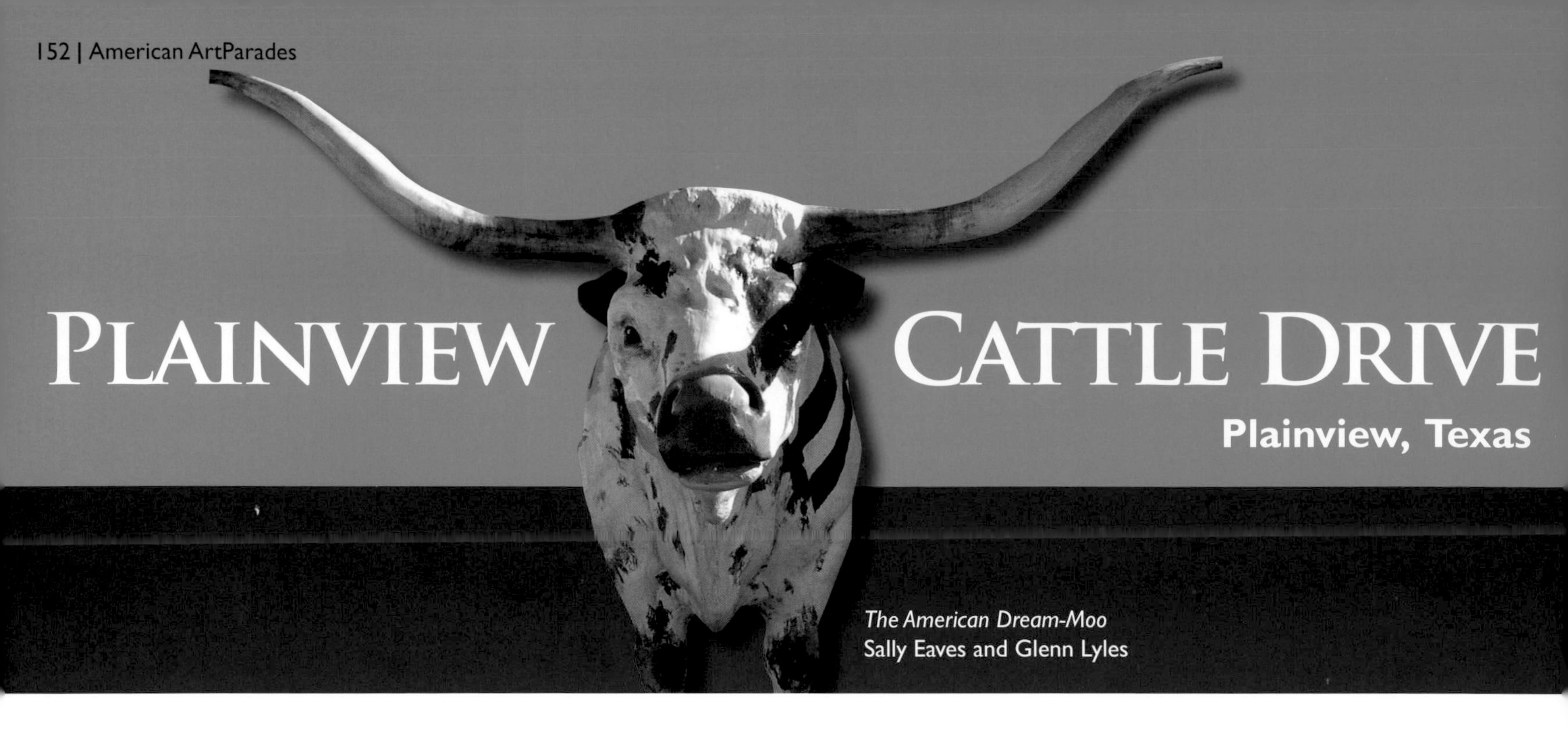

Plainview Cattle Drive

Plainview, Texas

The American Dream-Moo
Sally Eaves and Glenn Lyles

Plainview has a rich heritage in the cattle industry, and cattle drives have been an enduring part of its agricultural history. However, a new generation of cattle drive appeared on the horizon in the form of a fiberglass herd of brilliantly painted cattle that miraculously appeared at strategic locations throughout the city. And from that moment forward, the view was anything but plain.

Bovines with such amusing names as "Remember the Alamoo," "Holy Cow," and "Dairy Queen" grazed in parks and in front of businesses.

The *Plainview Cattle Drive* was a wonderful way for the entire family to experience this part of America, and it distinguished Plainview from other West Texas towns.

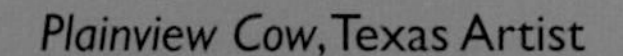

Plainview Cow, Texas Artist

Remember the Alamoo, Becky Smith

Savings Steer, Rodney Watson

Lone Steer, Candace Keller

"A NEW GENERATION OF CATTLE DRIVES APPEARED ON A CRISP SPRING MORNING."

Reef Beef, Ann Pollard

Our Hardwork Heritage, Rob Gould

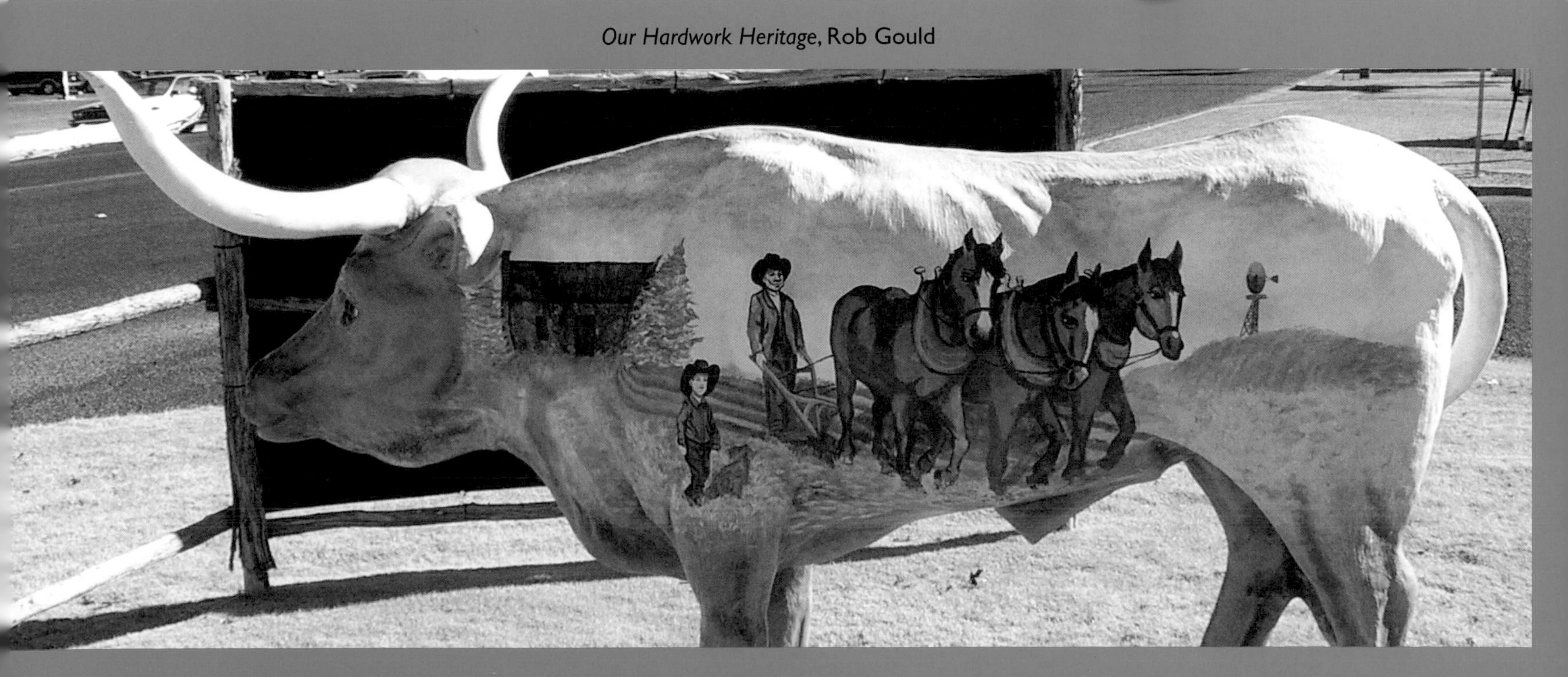

Seagull Fest

Salt Lake City, Utah

Paisely Princess
Bad Dog Rediscovers America

"Many visitors, and more locals than one would think, don't understand the significance of the seagull to Salt Lake City."

Mr. and Mrs. C. Gull, Dorian Soper

Gulls Night Out
Suzzo

A Day in the Park
Mary Brooks

Glamour Gull
Dorian Soper

The seagull is the Utah State bird, due to its heroic saving of the crops of Utah's first pioneers from a cricket infestation. Many visitors, and more locals than one would think, don't understand the significance of the seagull and crickets, and one objective of *Seagull Fest* was to provide an ongoing opportunity to educate everyone to this unique footnote in Utah's history, while creating a wonderful new folk art in the process.

Launched by a local artist and gallery director who were inspired by public art projects elsewhere, and who had a vision of people crowding the downtown streets to enjoy these whimsical creatures, *Seagull Fest* succeeded in both enriching community spirit and boosting the local economy. It also raised funds for youth art programs including the Utah Arts Alliance and Avenues For the Artz.

Left, top to bottom: *It's a Bird! It's a Plane!*, James "Torg" Torgersen, *Seagoyl*, Shauna Sudbury

Riding the Waves, Renee Shaw

Van Gull, Linda Bergstrom's Class

Guth, James "Torg" Torgersen

The Road Home, Bryan Travis

Salt Lake Bomber, Mary Brooks

Show Gull
Misty Rowan

Skater Gull
Linda Bergstrom and Midvale Elementary School

The Best Fish are Deep
Bryan Travis

THE UTAH BUFFALO ROUND-UP

Davis County
Weber County
Salt Lake County
Box Elder County
Summit County
Wasatch County
UTAH

Some of the American art parades were locally focused, while others were designed to attract outsiders. The organizers behind *The Utah Buffalo Round-up* had a larger audience in mind when they invited artists to turn fifty-two, life-size buffalo into eye-catching artworks.

Yes, they wanted to boost community spirit and pride. Yes, when the time came to auction these artistic tributes to "the great monarch of the North American plains" that once roamed through the valleys of Northern Utah, they wanted to raise money for local causes. But they also wanted to put themselves on the world map. And the way they planned to do that was use the 2002 Winter Olympics as their "gallery."

This was why, if you watched the Olympics on TV, you saw painted buffalos roaming the streets of Salt Lake City, the State Capitol grounds, and prominent places within Olympic Square. A white buffalo was even placed at the Utah Media Center for visiting dignitaries and Olympic medalists to autograph. Literally thousands of photographs were taken of these delightful creations, and both national and international media wrote stories about the project, with some television broadcasts using shots of the buffalo as a lead to news stories about the Olympic Games.

Sponsored by the Davis County Council of Governments, in addition to an immeasurable amount of publicity *The Utah Buffalo Round-up* raised over $100,000. for such deserving local organizations as The Friends of Antelope Island, Make-A-Wish Foundation, and the Davis Arts Council.

Where the Buffalo Roam
Blair Lewis and Kent Maxield

'59 Bull-Dorado
Mike Schaf
(crew: Gary Jenson
John Russell)

The Hand of Man Buffalo
Royden Card

Buffalore
John Kirkland

"The buffalo is an icon of the United States and the settling of the western reaches of the country."

Llamas of Lludlow

Ludlow, Vermont

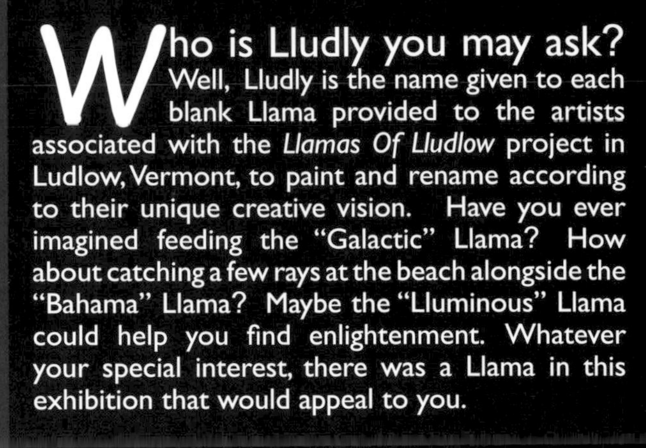

Who is Lludly you may ask? Well, Lludly is the name given to each blank Llama provided to the artists associated with the *Llamas Of Lludlow* project in Ludlow, Vermont, to paint and rename according to their unique creative vision. Have you ever imagined feeding the "Galactic" Llama? How about catching a few rays at the beach alongside the "Bahama" Llama? Maybe the "Lluminous" Llama could help you find enlightenment. Whatever your special interest, there was a Llama in this exhibition that would appeal to you.

More than thirty artists contributed to the collection of at least thirty-eight Llovable Llamas; one Llama was even painted by the art students of Lludlow Elementary School. Each Llama was adopted (sponsored) by a corporation, community group, or by private citizens and displayed around the community. Finally, the Llamas were auctioned off and the bulk of the proceeds given to Ludlow Streetscapes, a non-profit organization focusing on improving Lludlow. The balance of the proceeds went to support the Ludlow Artists Guild.

The Llamas of Lludlow project was not just a fantastic boon to the community, but a true celebration to be embraced by Llama lovers everywhere.

Below, left to right:
Cleo, Ludlow Elementary School Students
Llovable, Kim Ray
Llamadelic, Margo Goida
Americana, Donald Hofer
Four Seasons, Jeff Berkey
Arco Iris, Jiyl Y. Gilmour
Picasso, Cow Painters

“Our goal is to provide a fun, eye-catching community project.”

Below from left: *Llama Bean,* June Weber, *Big Sky,* William Nye, *Rustic Lady,* Laurie Marechaux, *Lluminous,* Barbara Storrs

A HORSE *Affair* Manchester Center, Vermont

American Beauty
Dave Herzfeld
Birch Blaze
June Heffernan
Race for the Cure
Jean Chau
The Fairy's Garden
Kimberley Ray
Parallax Pinto
Betsy Byrne Hubner
Halo
Vicki Lynn Bowden
Ol' 1856
Natalee Everett
From Seas to Shining Sea
Cynthia Rosen
Sea Horse
Anharad Llewlyn Edson
Galloping Gallery
Burr and Burton Students
Phlox Trot
Susan Sargent
Ethan Allen
Heather Bischoff
Godspeed
Ian Jamieson
Silent Flight
Scott Lenhardt
Season Delights
Susan Houghton-Debus
High Country Equine
Jinna McHugh

Glory Rose
Suzanne Little-Stefanik

Shadow Dancer
Pamela Marron

"Some stood, some grazed, others reared, but each and every horse was a true and original work of art, and the overall effect bedazzled."

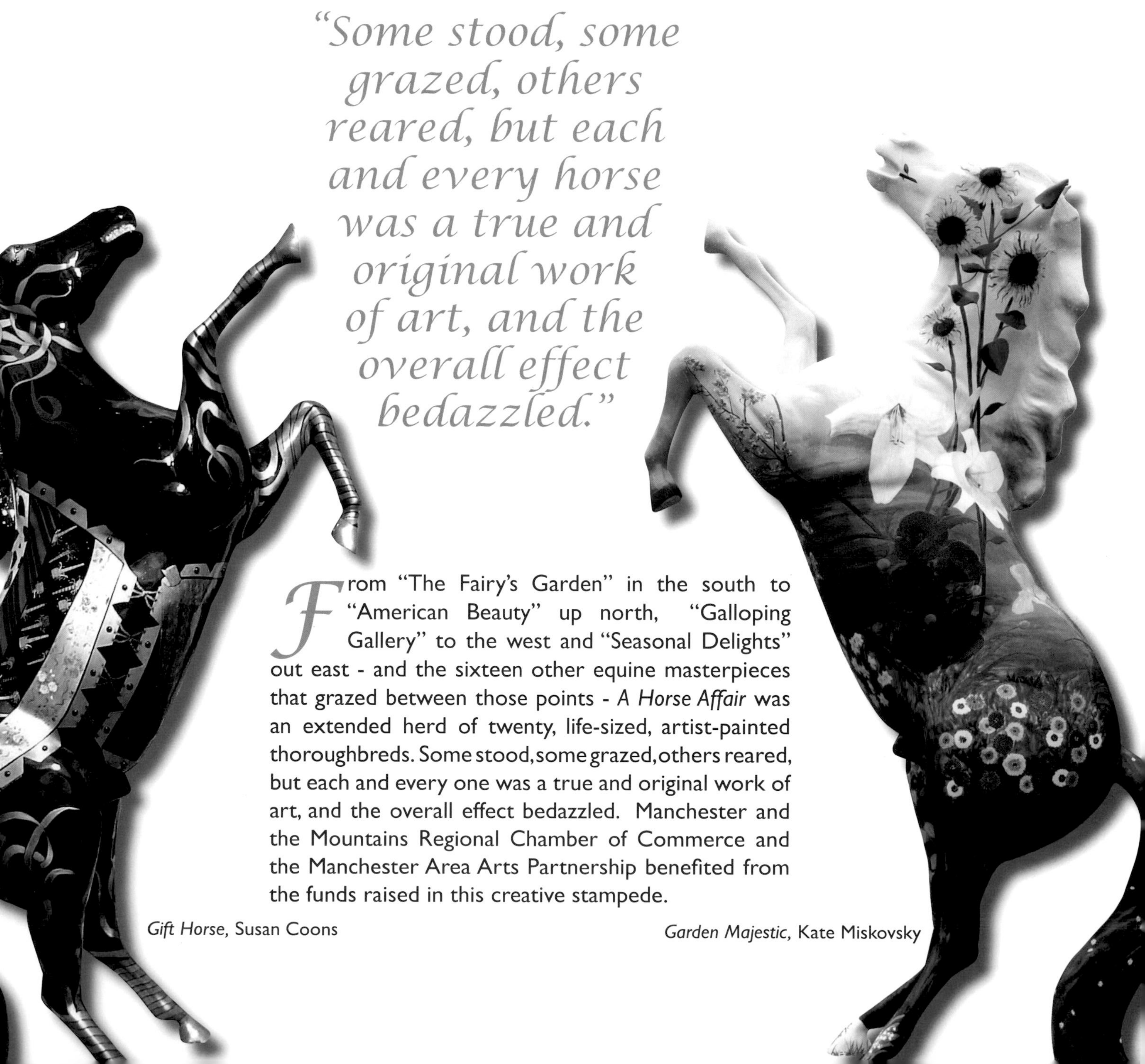

From "The Fairy's Garden" in the south to "American Beauty" up north, "Galloping Gallery" to the west and "Seasonal Delights" out east - and the sixteen other equine masterpieces that grazed between those points - *A Horse Affair* was an extended herd of twenty, life-sized, artist-painted thoroughbreds. Some stood, some grazed, others reared, but each and every one was a true and original work of art, and the overall effect bedazzled. Manchester and the Mountains Regional Chamber of Commerce and the Manchester Area Arts Partnership benefited from the funds raised in this creative stampede.

Gift Horse, Susan Coons

Garden Majestic, Kate Miskovsky

Pawsitively Fredericksburg!

Fredericksburg, Virginia

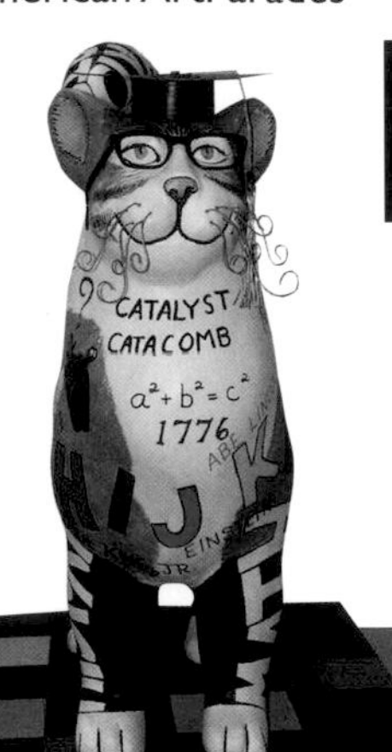

Educat, Susan C. Hill and Elaine Lavelle

The Fredricksburg National Historic District and hundreds of 18th and 19th century buildings were transformed into a playground featuring artistically decorated cats and dogs. Welcome to *Pawsitively Fredericksburg!*

The history of this charming Civil War city is larger than life, and so these works of art had to be larger than life in both size and subject. Artists were encouraged to create fanciful, flamboyant and unique companions that had "Pawsitive Personalities," many of which had relevance to Fredricksburg's past: "Clawbert E. Lee," "Colonial Calico," and "Rappahannock Mews," to name a few.

Pawsitively Fredricksburg! celebrated the "Pawsitive Creativity" of the local arts community and thousands of visitors enjoyed this extraordinary exhibition which benefited the Historic Fredricksburg Foundation and many deserving local organizations.

Watch-Dog, Hsi-Mei Yates

Golden Retriever, Andrea Shreve Taylor

Picatso, Trista Depp Chapman

Dogwood, Linda Warshaw

Poppy Cat, Betsy Glassie

Woof Down a Good Book, Faith Broome

Rappahannock Mews, Jean Lauzon

Delftware Kitty, Milvi K. Gill

"These works of art were larger than life in both size and subject."

Paws to Reflect, Susan E. Hernandez

Mermaids On Parade

Norfolk, Virginia

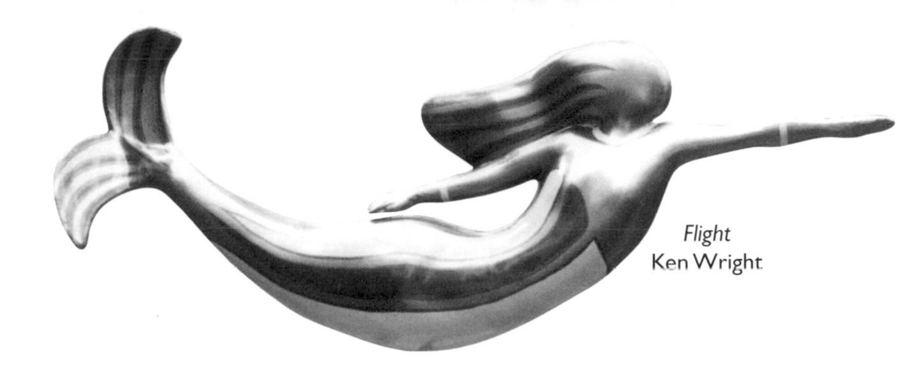

Flight
Ken Wright

Tiger Woods at a golf tournament featuring *Mermaids on Parade*.

One summer, it was almost as if a magical tidal wave washed over this seaport town, leaving behind more than a hundred sirens of legend on the sidewalks and in the parks. A pair of mermaids made of mirrors reflected the sun back onto the faces of passersby; a mermaid trailing copper locks greeted sailors coming into port; a mermaid wearing the painted "cloth" of West Africa brightened one of the City's historic buildings undergoing renovation.

Some mermaids were funny, such as the one wrapped as a chocolate candy bar – with a bite out of her tail. Three were electric – lighting the night with their bold colors. They were regal, playful and somber; they celebrated life, local attractions, and causes from literacy to regional cooperation. One traveled to Virginia Beach trailing stars – dedicated to the "individual spirits and determination to live independent lives" of people with disabilities.

This spectacular gathering arrived in a year when Norfolk was celebrating the culmination of a decades-long effort to revitalize its downtown core. And in addition to injecting color and humor into the community and giving visitors and residents a reason to explore the improvements to this "new" port city, the mermaids became, in the words of a local columnist, "grace notes lifting spirits" into a new century, while providing support for local art projects and non-profit organizations.

Silver Mermaid
Liz Greene and William E. Wood

Evening Seagoddess
Michele Barnes

Spectrum Gold
Michele Barnes

Catch of the Day
Terry Cox-Joseph

Yuma Ya
Dave Iwans

"The mermaids were regal, playful and somber; they celebrated life, local attractions and causes."

Shellina
Maury High School
Judy Saunders

W.H. Taylor Elementary School

Kevin Gallup, Sculptor

Myke Irving, Artist

Debbie Small, Artist

Heart of the Sea
Sandra Singletary

APPLES ON PARADE

Winchester and Frederick County, Virginia

Seeds of Wisdom
Mary Stedwill Rabai

Small Images above left to right, top to bottom: *Bites of Local Life*, Katrina Hawes, *Eve*, Michael Graves & Associates, *Air White House*, E. Marie Solbien, *Kimberly's Apple*, Local Artists, *Windows to the World of Agriculture*, Anna Golladay and McIntosh Creative Design, *Bites of Winchester*, Bryan Fleming and Sky High Productions, *A Taste of History*, Honors Art Students at Daniel Morgan Middle School, *An Apple a Day...*, Marketing Department, Valley Health System, *Welcome PineApple*, Jen Krock, *World's Safest Apple*, T. Mark Poole

"As you drive around the community 'picking' out the apples, you'll see the unbelievable talent of local artists come alive on a unique canvas."

Starry Night Over the Shenandoah Valley
Anna Golladay,
McIntosh Creative Design

Expanding Tradition
Virgil K. Austin

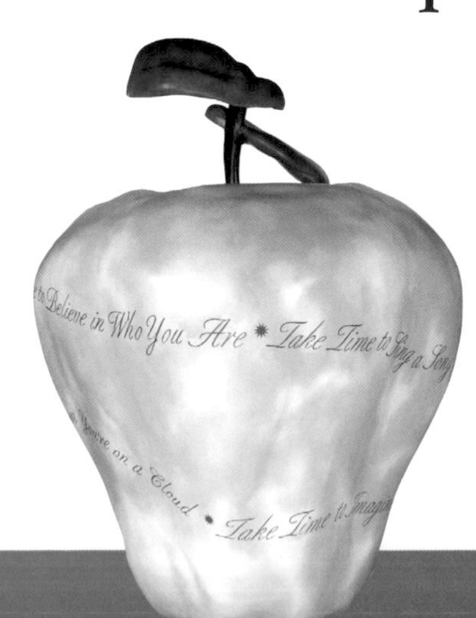

The Sky's The Limit
Jennifer Bright Blazek,
Legacy Wall Designs

Stars and Stripes of Winchester –Frederick County
Mike Harden, Jr, Harden Graphic

A Most Tasteful 1, Radford Wine

If an apple a day keeps the doctor away, then you can be sure that there wasn't a sneeze or a sniffle within a hundred miles of Winchester-Frederick County, Virginia during *Apples on Parade*.

Nestled in the Shenandoah Valley, this is a community overflowing with historic allure and captivating beauty. A community that shaped a young George Washington, that brought the world greatness like Willa Cather and Patsy Cline, and that was so pivotal to our Civil War that it reportedly changed hands more than 70 times.

The Shenandoah Valley also happens to be the sixth largest apple producer in the country, which explains why, when the Convention and Visitors Bureau decided to team up with the Chamber of Commerce to celebrate the community's heritage, they selected 8-foot tall, 6-foot wide apples to be "polished" by Virginia artists.

From depictions of historic figures to spectacular panoramas, every apple shouted out a celebration of all that is special about Winchester and Frederick County. And in the fall, when the apples were "harvested," a bushel of money was raised for local philanthropic organizations.

Apple Pi
John Handley High School's Drawing and Painting I Class

Seattle, Washington

"The Chinese 'Year of the Pig' marks the return of *Pigs on Parade* to Pike Place Market."

Madame Fleur de Piglette
Karen Kohtz

April Showers
Fitzgerald DeFreitas

When Pigs Fly
Selina Kwan

As the animal-parade fever heated up across the country, Seattle went hog wild. More than one hundred and sixty fiberglass pigs took up residence on city streets in the form of *Pigs on Parade,* which was produced by The Pike Place Market Foundation. The inspiration was Rachel, a life-size bronze piggy bank that for many years had stood proudly at the entrance to the historic Pike Place Market, bringing home the bacon by raising money for needy families and seniors in the area.

Seattle area artists, residents and businesses, such as Starbucks, came together as a community to support *Pigs on Parade*. Soon there was an oink oink here, an oink oink there, everywhere an oink oink in downtown Seattle. Beautifully decorated pigs paraded through the city streets delighting visitors and residents with their barnyard behavior.

Any pig wrangler knows what a slippery business it is to round up a herd of pigs. But that's exactly what happened at a "Wine, Swine and Dine" gala and auction that brought the "piggest event" in Seattle history to a close. The entire community squealed with such delight after raising over $500,000. to support The Pike Place Market Foundation, that they decided to mark the "Year of the Pig" with the "Return of the Pigs."

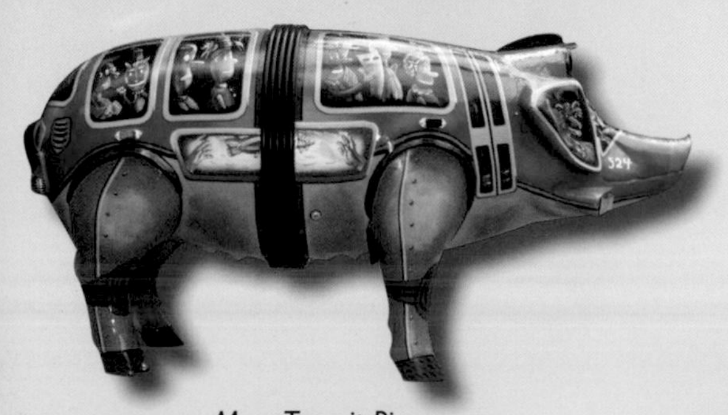

Mass Transit Pig
Robert Massa

Pork Chopper
Colin Reedy and Luisa Herrera

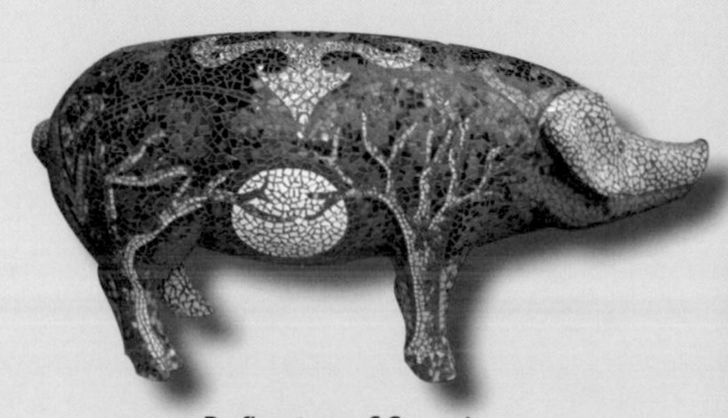

Reflection of Sound
Elaine Summers

Totem Pig
Jack Kleinart, Marcus, Nolan, Wyatt and Mickey

Ballpark Frank
Lane Gwinn

Porca
Jenny Pohlman, Jeanne Brennan and Sabrina Knowles

Cochon Et Chinoiserie
Karen Knaus

Pigasso
Dawn Isaacs

Raj Pig
Starbucks Visual Group

Ball Hog
Lisa Gardner, R.K. Cobban and Andy Costabel

Porca Sitting
Langley Middle School, 6th through 8th Graders

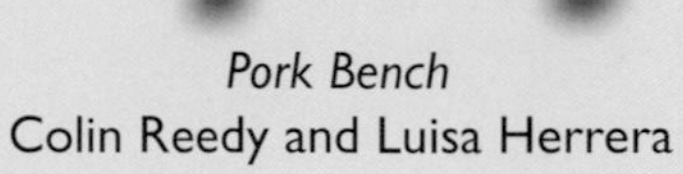

Pork Bench
Colin Reedy and Luisa Herrera

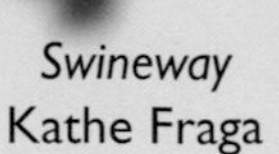

Swineway
Kathe Fraga

Bellevue
Leavenworth
Mount Vernon
Olympia
Orcas Island
Port Angeles
Port Townsend
Seattle
Tacoma
WASHINGTON

SOUL SALMON

"Art can stop you in your tracks like nothing else! Imagine coming to work one day and being startled by an 8-foot salmon you would meet only in a dream. It might be wearing a hat, sporting flames, sprouting trees or cloaked in poems praising rivers. Imagine the effect of hundreds of such salmon throughout the state!"

So wrote TAHMANAWIS, the non-profit entity that sponsored the project called *Soul Salmon*. Their mission? "To nourish Pacific Northwest arts, education, ecologic restoration and culture by encouraging periodic, spirited 'art actions' that celebrate, interpret and re-imagine the natural world that sustains us all and generate charity to save native salmon."

Celestial Luna Lox
Sara Mall Johani

Pugent Sound Explorer
Jon Soini

Spawned Out King
Rainey Daze

Native Soul Family
Loren White, Steve Brown and Lane Quine

Save the Last Dance for Me
Ela Brickson

"ART CAN STOP YOU IN YOUR TRACKS LIKE NOTHING ELSE."

Mojo Mariners
Karen Moyers

Wrong Way Finnegan
Lynn Di Nino

ICU
Chimacum Creek Printing

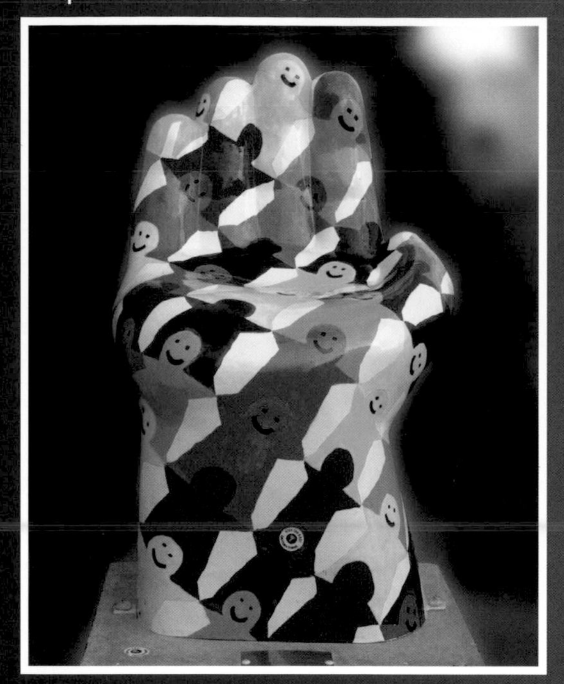

Hand Me A Smile, Grace Binder

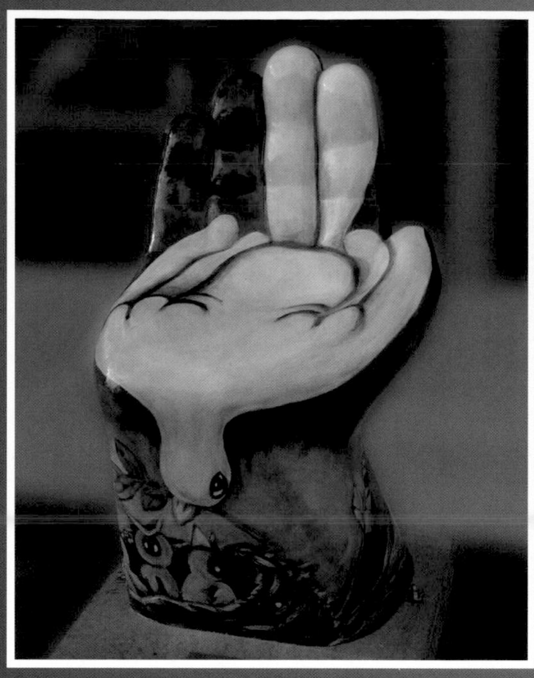

A Bird In Hand, Cyndee Kaiser

Carmen Miranda Sat Here, Laurie Bieze

Hands Across Eau Claire

Eau Claire, Wisconsin

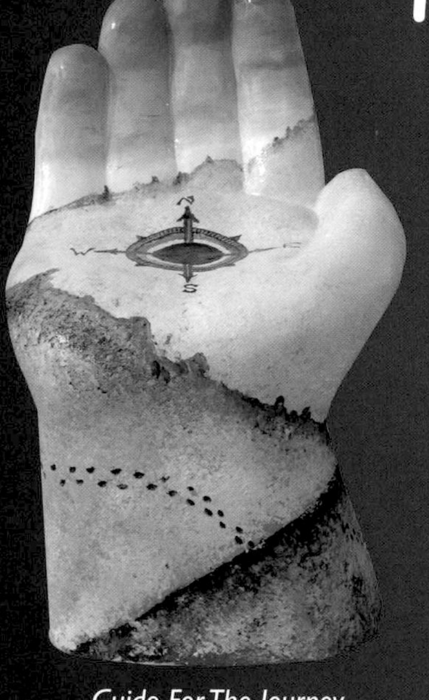

Guide For The Journey
Lara Guetsch

At the Children's Museum of Eau Claire, the mission is to create "an interactive environment for children and grown-ups that inspires imagination, discovery, creativity and the love of learning." The museum took a hands-on approach to the streets when it decided to follow the lead from other towns with their own creative event designed to entice visitors and locals to get involved with public art. The hand was an obvious choice for many reasons. Not only was the hand the logo for the museum, but a hand is also a symbol of helping, reaching out, learning and friendship.

Hands Across Eau Claire featured twenty-five sculpted hands exhibited throughout the community, each 42-inches tall and 20-inches wide. Creatively decorated by local artists, these extended hands reminded people that the Children's Museum of Eau Claire was a great place for hands-on learning and an experience that was worthy of their support.

Handful Of Friends
Patricia Mayhew Hamm

Backyard Fun
Janelle Isaacson

Cow Hand
Angela Zank

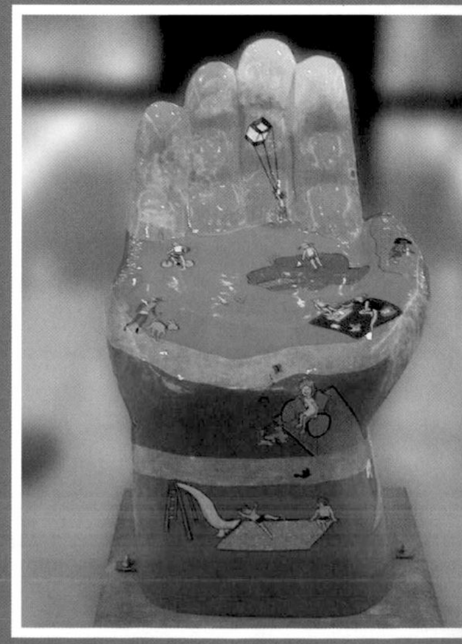

Best Playground Hand
Patti and Jade Kettenacker

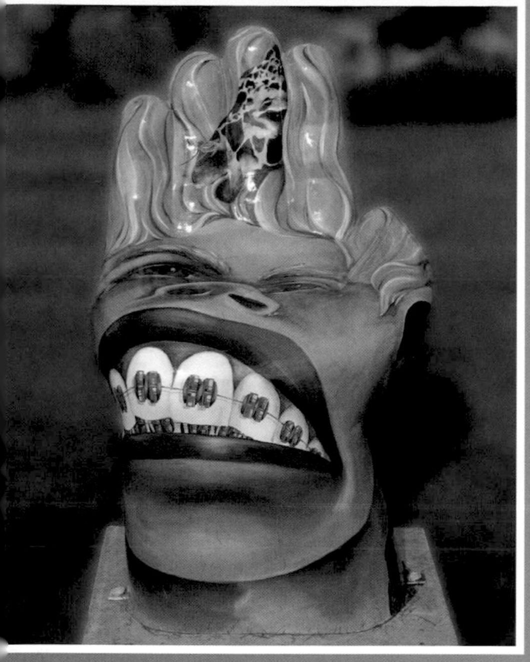

Heavy Metal, Stacey Carlson-Kelly

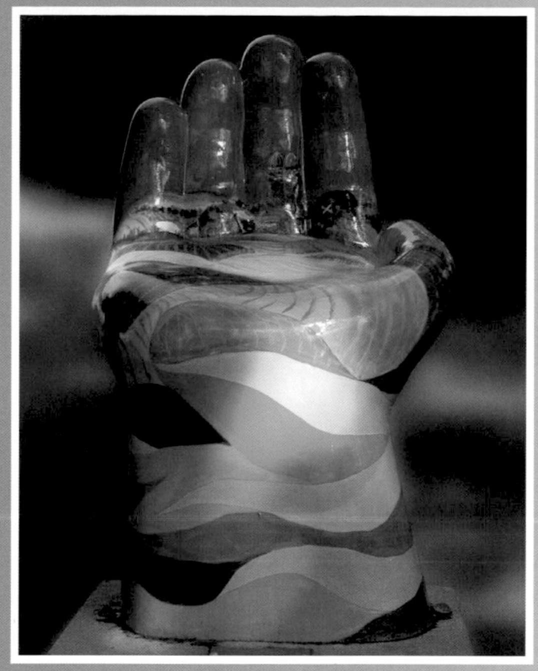

Wisconsin Farmland, Jo Burke

Your Imagination Can Reach Anywhere, Kelly Zmuda

"A hand is a symbol of helping, reaching out, learning and friendship."

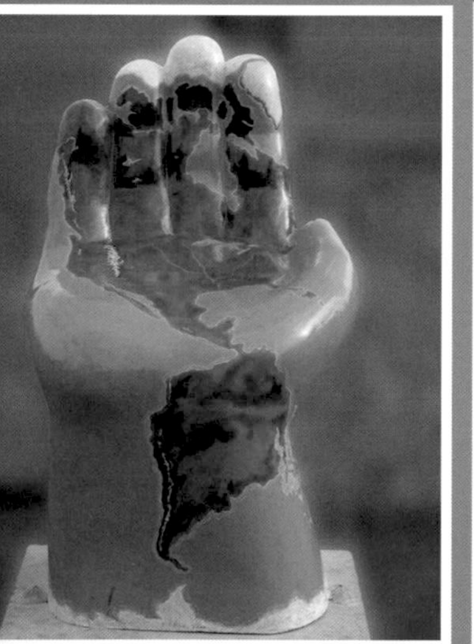

Without Borders
Tiit Raid

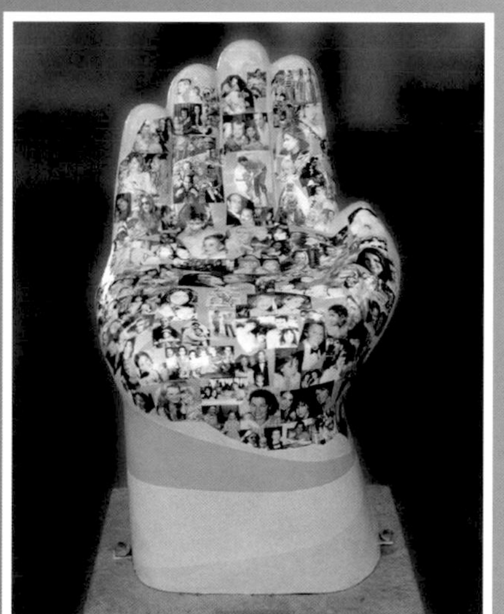

Faces
Richard Weld

Mother's Hand
Susan Eaton

Floral Hand
Barbara Shafer

Hands Through History
Alisa Goetch

Time On Your Hands
Jean Young

Lumberjacks In Woodgrain
Andy Shafer

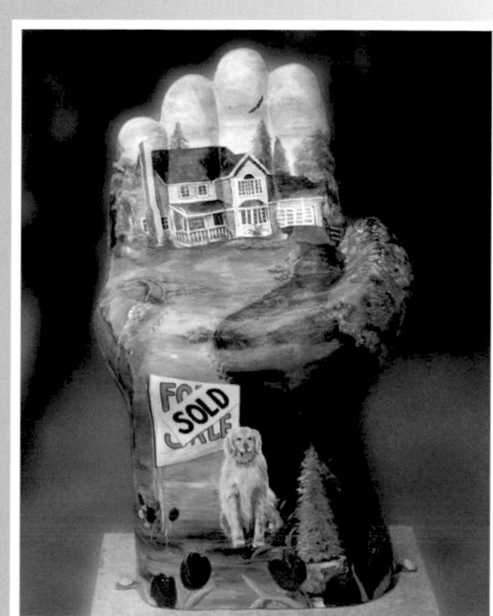

Sold
Janelle Isaacson

BEASTIE BEAT™

Milwaukee, Wisconsin

While communities and organizations elsewhere themed their art projects on a universally recognizable animal or icon, Milwaukee turned to a creature born and bred locally. Created in the 1960s by artist Dennis Pearson, the Beastie is an amorphous, four-legged form with a long neck and head that resembles a horse/dog/dinosaur cross while retaining its own identity… an identity that invites viewers to inventively transform it into a creature of their own imagination. It was the perfect fit for a project that appealed to fertile minds, and the results were notable. Beasties sang, strummed and snorkeled throughout the city and became so loved by the community that an encore presentation took place.

The majority of the Beasties were designed according to musical themes because *Beastie Beat*™ was conceived as a project that would help reposition Milwaukee in the national consciousness as an exciting performing arts community. Once known as "The Machine Shop of the World" and the "Beer Capital," Milwaukee has reinvented itself. *Beastie Beat*™ has brought awareness of this new arts mecca while raising money to support the Milwaukee Symphony Orchestra and its nationally heralded Youth Music Education programs.

Summer Breeze
Dennis Pearson

Hot! Hot! Hot!
Julie Trump

Lions and Tigers and Beasties, Oh My
Dan Szczepanski

It Ain't Over 'Til the Fat Lady Sings
Anita Burgermeister

"BEASTIES SANG, STRUMMED AND SNORKELED THROUGHOUT THE CITY."

Lyndee's Carnival of Animals
Dee Dee Pellegrin
Lynn Delzer

Suba-Duba-Doo
Dan Augustine
Chris Bishop Seramur

Cat'n Around Downtown

Downtown Bears It All

Downtown Summer Splash

Racine, Wisconsin

D*og Days of Summer. Cat'n Around Downtown. Downtown Bears It All. Downtown Summer Splash.* What do all these public art projects have in common? They helped in the renaissance of downtown Racine, Wisconsin.

Situated on the shores of Lake Michigan between Chicago and Milwaukee, Racine's downtown experienced the challenges that many cities eventually encounter…how to bring energy, vitality and commercial businesses back to the city center. During the1980's, community efforts were initiated to reinvigorate the downtown and public art began to play a major role. Large works of art by local artists dotted the streets and essentially invited residents and visitors to re-discover Racine. These exhibitions were different and exciting and people developed a whole new sense of pride and community spirit that continues to be felt today.

Racine has demonstrated its commitment to public art and redevelopment. They have also generated an invaluable awareness of the power of the arts and the importance of downtown redevelopment, while raising needed funds for The Racine Art Museum and the Racine Heritage Museum.

"Public art will continue in Downtown Racine. It has proven to be a real attraction..."

Hakuna Mutt
Tatta, Sue Horton

Darth-Otter, Jerry Treiber

Scully, Sybil Brauneis Klug

Something's Fishy
Tammy Easton

Bob Cat, Don Bugalecki

Images right, top to bottom:
Ivory Billed Woodpecker Visits Racine
Bill Reid
Lions and Tigers and Bears, Oh My!
Angela Perrault
Bean E. Bear
Jeff Levonian
Grin and Bear It
Karen, Krista and
Becca Johnson

Hide and Seek
Kathleen Lippold

The Cat's in the Ladle
Randall Underwood

THESE BOOTS are made for TALKING

Cheyenne, Wyoming

"A lot of famous boots with spurs a jinglin' have made their way from the train platform onto the streets of Cheyenne."

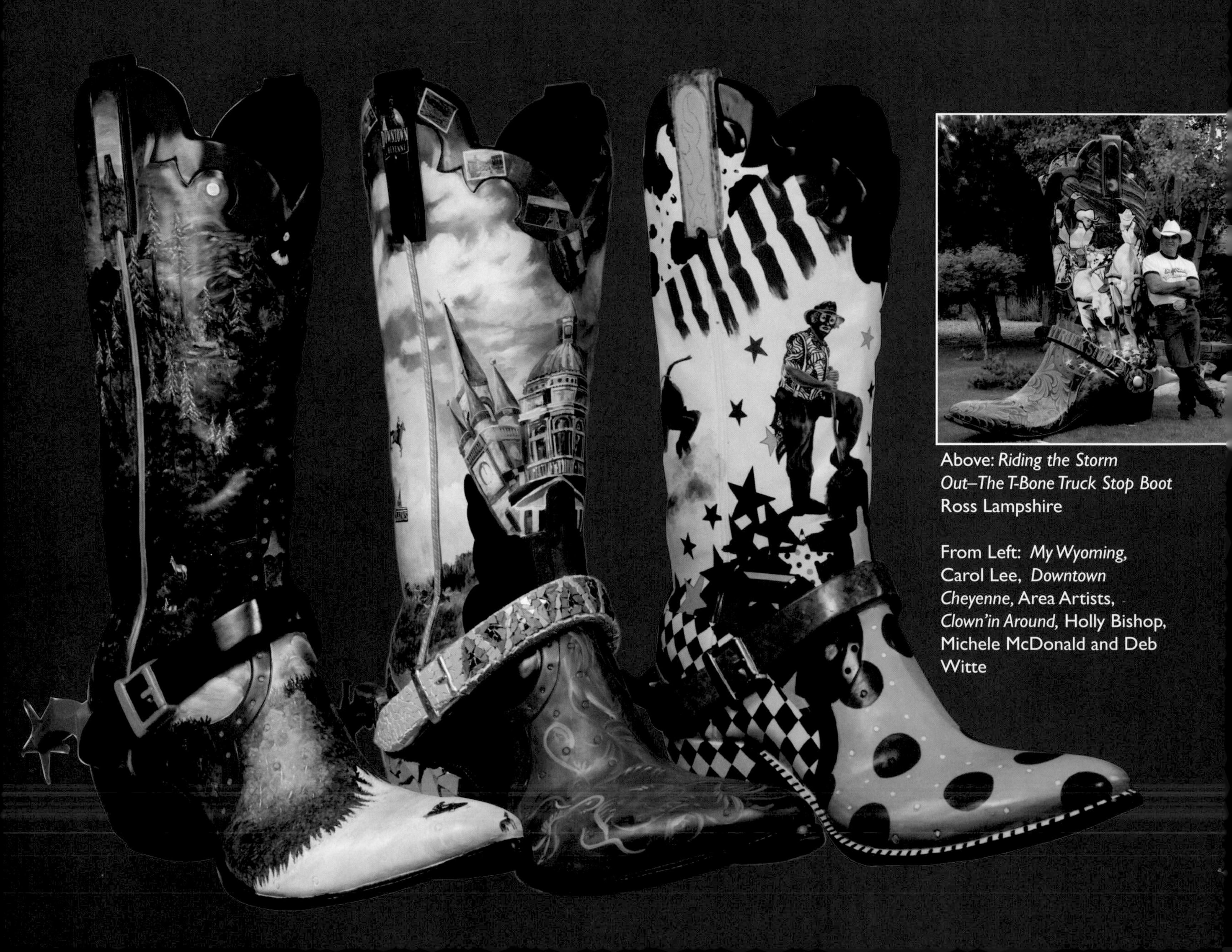

Above: *Riding the Storm Out–The T-Bone Truck Stop Boot* Ross Lampshire

From Left: *My Wyoming*, Carol Lee, *Downtown Cheyenne*, Area Artists, *Clown'in Around*, Holly Bishop, Michele McDonald and Deb Witte

Above, left to right:
Memories of the Old West, Cody Hamil, *Get Along Little Doggies*, Karen Henneck and Ginny Butcher, *Blue Skies Over Cheyenne*, John Gutherie, *Outlaws of Wyoming*, Cheyenne Artist Guild, *Perils of the Expressman*, Art Kober, *Rhinestone Cowboy*, Sue Miller, *Fishin' Boot*, Terri Thurman, *Cowboy/Cowgirl Boot*, Jerry Palen, *Red Bandanna*, Karen Buck, *8 Second Steps To The Big Time*, Ross Lampshire, *Springtime In Cheyenne*, Rose Burrows, *Saga of Tom Horn*, Cecil Burnett

The Union Pacific Depot has been and remains an important part of the history of Cheyenne and Wyoming. A lot of famous boots with spurs a jinglin' have made their way from the train platform at the Union Pacific Depot, across the lobby's original stone floor, and then onto the streets of Cheyenne. Included are the boots of the Earp brothers, Wild Bill Hickock, Buffalo Bill Cody, Doc Holiday, Tom Horn, Teddy Roosevelt, Molly Brown and General Pershing, to name just a few. So it made perfect sense that when the Cheyenne Depot Museum Foundation and the Downtown Development Authority decided to pair up and put on a public art project, their theme would be "If this boot could talk, what story would it tell?"

The 8-foot tall boots were decorated by artists from across the state of Wyoming and ran the gamut from humorous to sweet, from historic to modern. Their purpose was to foster the economic and physical enhancement of downtown Cheyenne and ensure the future operational success of the Cheyenne Depot Museum, and they did just that.

Images left, top to bottom: *Wyoming Cowboy Tough*, Chris Navarro, *Religion's a Kick*, Mike McIntosh

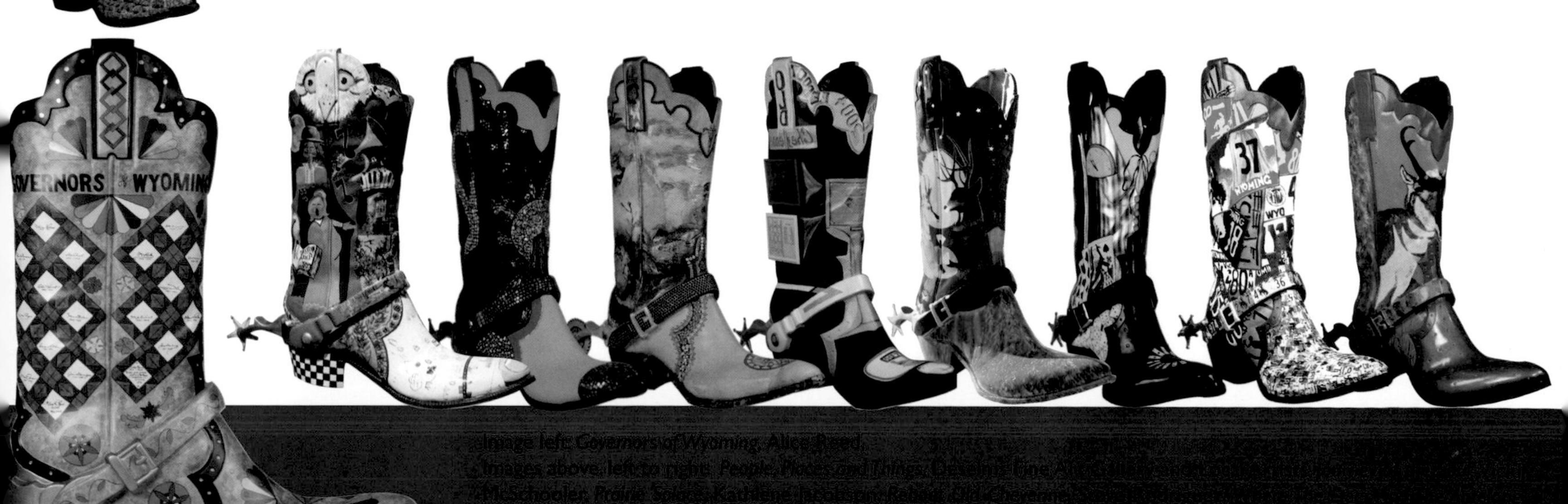

Image left: *Governors of Wyoming*, Alice Reed,
Images above, left to right: *People, Places and Things*, [illegible] McSchooler, *Prairie Solace*, Kathlene Jacobsen, *Rebel Old Cheyenne* [illegible] *Play*, Liz Gaagy, *Gamblers Boot*, Max Larkin, [illegible] Lahiff

AMERICAN
ARTPARADES

WHEN PIGS FLEW, GUITARS ROCKED
AND COWS JUMPED OVER THE MOON
It's Not The End...
It's Only The Beginning!

Grants Pass "BearFest," Grants Pass, Oregon

Geckos in Paradise, Honolulu, Hawaii

Wild Salmon on Parade, Anchorage, Alaska

Acknowledgements

First of all, we would like to express our appreciation to all of the organizations referred to in this book, who not only worked so hard to put on art parades in their communities, but who generously provided us with pictorial and textual material so that we could honor their efforts in *American ArtParades*. We must also acknowledge their extraordinary accomplishments in raising funds for deserving philanthropic organizations, the environment and downtown redevelopment. To date, tens of millions of dollars have been generated by these American art parades.

We would like to thank Mr. Nathan Mason, Curator of Special Projects, Public Art Program, Department of Cultural Affairs, City of Chicago, for penning the preface to American ArtParades. We would also like to thank Mr. Dennis B. Sprung, President and CEO of the American Kennel Club, Ms. Dorothy McSweeny, Chairperson, Board of Commissioners for the DC Commission on the Arts and Humanities and Mr. Tony Gittens, Executive Director of the DC Commission on the Arts and Humanities, Washington DC, and Ms. Bryn Wilkins from *The Trail of Painted Ponies* for their efforts and support.

We are especially indebted to the participating artists who shared their creativity with us, the writers who described these projects in ways that added to our enjoyment and understanding, and the photographers who created a stunning visual record. But virtually all of these public art projects had their share of behind-the-scenes players that included community members, businesses, and individuals. Without their contributions the projects never would have taken place, and we would like to sincerely thank each and every one of them.

We would also like to salute the philanthropic organizations that benefited from these art parades. In many cases, these organizations had to become full working partners with their communities and to that end, had to develop new business skills to succeed. These non-profit organizations are invaluable to communities and often toil in obscurity, so it has been a distinct pleasure to highlight their important work.

Finally, extraordinary efforts were made to locate and contact organizations and communities in every state in the nation that produced public art projects and invite them to be part of *American ArtParades*. This proved to be a daunting task. Many parades had moved on and many individuals who organized these events had returned to their jobs or other projects. *American ArtParades*, therefore, is a tribute to each and *every* public art parade that has taken place across America. Congratulations and thank you, all.

Karlynn Keyes
Vice President
The Trail of Painted Ponies, Inc.

Creator/Director
The Gallery at Four Seasons Resort Scottsdale

Rod Barker
President
The Trail of Painted Ponies, Inc.

DIRECTORY

ALABAMA
Dothan
Peanuts Around Town
www.thedowntowngroup.com
111 North St. Andrees Street
Dothan AL 36303-4837
Contact: Cathy Cole
Executive Director
of the Downtown Group
334 793-3097
Photography: Nick Stakelum,
The Image Agency

ALASKA
Anchorage
Wild Salmon on Parade
www.wildsalmononparade.com
P.O. Box 143451
Anchorage AK 99514
Contact: Melinda Taylor
907 777-7248
mtaylor@ibew1547.org
Photography: Wild Salmon on Parade

ARIZONA
Carefree
The Trail of Painted Ponies Inc.
www.trailofpaintedponies.com
P.O. Box 2629
Carefree AZ 85377-2629
Contact: Bryn Wilkins/
Karlynn Keyes
480 459-5700
Bryn@trailofpaintedponies.com
Karlynn@trailofpaintedponies.com
Photography: Eduardo Fuss, Don Bell
and Bryn Wilkins at The Trail of Painted
Ponies

CALIFORNIA
Palm Springs
Path of the Bighorn®
www.pathofthebighorn.com
425 Via Lola
Palm Springs CA 92262
Contact: Alexandra Sheldon
760 320-2909
Monetrenoirsasha@aol.com
Photography: Taylor Sherrill

Sacramento
Lions on Safari
www.saczoo.com
Sacramento Zoo
3930 West Land Park Drive
Sacramento CA 95822
Contact: Mary Healy
CEO/Director Sacramento Zoo
916 808-5166
mhealy@cityofsacramento.org
Photography: Lions on Safari

San Diego
Urban Trees
www.portofsandiego.org
P.O. Box 488
San Diego CA 92112
Contact: Catherine Sass
619 686-6468
csass@portofsandiego.org
Photography: Port of San Diego Photos
and Raymond Elstad

San Francisco
Hearts in San Francisco
www.sfghf.net
San Francisco General
Hospital Foundation
2789 25th Street Suite 2028
San Francisco CA 94110
Contact: Katherine Moe
415 206-4478
info@sfghf.net
Photography: Bill Zemanek Photography

San Jose
SharkByte Art™
www.sjdowntown.com
San Jose Downtown
Association
28 N First Street 10th Floor
San Jose CA 95113
Contact: Rick Jensen
408 279-1775
rjensen@sjdowntown.com
Photography: Brian Eder
and Dana Grover

San Luis Obispo
Trout About Downtown
www.visitslo.com
1341 Nipomo Street
San Luis Obispo CA 93401
Contact: Betsy Kiser
Parks and Recreation Director
805 781-7299
bkiser@slocity.org
Photography: Barnett, Cox
and Associates

COLORADO
Colorado Springs
Ban Bare Bears
www.ppbhg.org
Pikes Peak Behavioral Health
Group
525 North Cascade Avenue
P.O. Box 15318
Colorado Springs CO 80935-5318
Contact: Cynthia K. Doty
719 314-4310
cynthiad@ppbhg.org
Photography: David Vesse

Durango
Pumas on Parade
www.sjma.org
SJMA
P.O. Box 2261
Durango CO 81302
Contact: Susan Bryson
970 385-1312
Susan@sjma.org
Photography: Scott DW Smith/
Imagesmith Photo

Longmont
Geese Galore
912 5th Avenue
Longmont CO 80501
Contact: Sandy Jensen
303 776-6943
sjensen@peakpeak.com
Photography: Dwyer Photography
and Terrance Repasky

CONNECTICUT
Darien, New Canaan, Norwalk, Wilton, Weston, and Westport
Galaxy of Stars
www.starinc-lightingtheway.org
182 Wolfpit Avenue
Norwalk CT 06851
Contact: Katie Banzhaf
203 846-9581 ext 304
kbanzhaf@starinconline.com
Photography: Katie J. Banzhaf

DELAWARE
Wilmington
Dino Days
Cool City Cars
Wilmington Wonderland
www.citylifewilmington.com
Wilmington Renaissance Corporation
214 North Market Street
Wilmington DE 19801
Contact: Carrie W. Gray
Managing Director
302 425-5500
wrc@bigplanet.com
Photography: Wilmington
Renaissance Corporation

DISTRICT OF COLUMBIA

Washington

Party Animals
Pandamania

www.partyanimals.org
www.pandamaniadc.org
DC Commission on the
Arts and Humanities
410 8th Street NW
Fifth Floor
Washington DC 20004
Contact: Tony Gittens
202 724-5613
tony.gittens@dc.gov
Photography: John Woo

FLORIDA

Key West

Dolphins on Parade™

www.keysarts.com
Florida Keys Council
of The Arts
1100 Simonton Street
Key West FL 33040
Contact: Monica Haskell
305 295-4369
info@keysarts.com
Photography: Sam Kennedy

GEORGIA

Athens

We Let the Dawgs Out

www.weletthedawgsout.org
1737-B South Lumpkin Street
Athens GA 30606
Contact: Linda Ford/Julie Walter
706 549-6843
dawgs@weletthedawgsout.org
Photography: We Let the Dawgs Out

Tybee Island

Tybee Turtle Tour

www.tybeeturtletour.org
P.O. Box 2344
Tybee Island GA 31328
Contact: Mary Ingalls
912 786-5920
turtles@rammb.com
Photography: Nancy Heffernen
and Rebecca Rice

HAWAII

Honolulu

Geckos In Paradise℠

www.geckosinparadise.com
Kapi'olani Health Foundation
55 Merchant Street 26th Floor
Honolulu HI 96813
Contact: Stacey Acma
808 535-7100
info@geckosinparadise.com
Photography: Alana Burrows

IDAHO

Coeur d'Alene

No Moose Left Behind

www.excelfoundation.org
EXCEL Foundation
P.O. Box 2469
Coeur d' Alene ID 83816
Contact: Heidi Rogers
208 292-2683
info@excelfoundation.org
Photography: Frank Martin

Hailey, Ketchum and Sun Valley

Summer of Labs
www.fortunatedogcookies.com
Contact: Terry Tischer/Lyn Stallard
208 726-6699
thatlyn@yahoo.com
Photography: Andy Hawley

ILLINOIS

Bloomington

Corn-on-the-Curb

www.downtownbloomington.org
107 West Market Street
Bloomington IL 61701
Contact: Marlene Gregor
309 828-8838
marlenegregor@aol.com
Photography: Lori Ann Cook

Chicago

Cows on Parade™ In Chicago
www.cityofchicago.org/culturalaffairs
Public Art Program
Department of Cultural Affairs
City of Chicago Cultural Center
78 East Washington Street
Chigcago IL 60602
Contact: Nathan Mason
Curator of Special Projects
312 742-1232
nathan.mason@cityofchicago.org
Photography: Department of Cultural
Affairs, City of Chicago

Elmhurst

Cool Kiddie Cars
www.coolkiddiecars.com
2 City Centre
Elmburst IL 60126
Contact: Deb Fredrickson
630 993-1600
deb@elmhurstcitycentre.com
Photography: Cool Kiddie Cars

Naperville

Magical Giving Garden;
Farmyard Friends
www.NapervilleUnitedWay.org
Naperville United Way
29 South Webster Street
Suite 106 B
Naperville IL 60540
Contact: Deena Manna
630 369-2676
dmanna@uw-mc.org
Photography: Magical Giving Garden
and Farmyard Friends

Zion

Adopt-A-Bee Program "Zion – A Great Place to Bee"
www.cityofzion.com
Adopt-A-Bee-Program
2828 Sheridan Road
Zion IL 60099
Contact: Delaine Rogers
847 746-4015
delainer@zion.il.us
Photography: Carla Villalobos

INDIANA

Fort Wayne

Mastodons on Parade
www.ipfwmastodons.org
2101 East Coliseum Blvd
Fort Wayne IN 46805-1499
Contact: Irene Walters
260 481-6104
walters@ipfw.edu
Photography: Randy Jackson

Indianapolis

Dolphins By Design
www.indianapoliszoo.com
Indianapolis Zoo
1200 West Washington Street
Indianapolis IN 46222
Contact: Judith Gagen
317 630-2010
Cell 317 523-4294
jgagen@indyzoo.com
Photography: Judith L. Gagen

IOWA

CEDAR RAPIDS

Overalls All Over
www.cedar-rapids.com
119 First Ave SE
Cedar Rapids IA 52401
Contact: Matt Krug
319 398-5009
mattkrug@cedar-rapids.com
Photography: Overalls All Over

SIOUX CITY

Prairie Dog
Discovery Dog
www.siouxcityartcenter.org
Sioux City Art Center
225 Nebraska Street
Sioux City IA 51101
Contact: Al Harris-Fernandez
712 279-6272
Photography: Scott Haberer and George Lindblade

KENTUCKY

LOUISVILLE

Gallopalooza
www.gallopaloozaderby.com
MetroCall
400 South First Street
Louisville KY 40202
502 574-5000
gallopalooza@aol.com
Photography: Dan Dry

LOUISIANA

LAKE CHARLES

Gators on the Geaux
www.lcsymphony.org
Lake Charles Symphony
P.O. Box 3102
Lake Charles LA 70602-3102
Contact: Debbie Reed
337 433-1611
info@lcsymphony.org
Photography: Gators on the Geaux

MAINE

BELFAST

Belfast Bearfest™
www.belfastbearfest.com
The City of Belfast
93 Main Street
Belfast ME 04915
Contact: Mayor Mike Hurley
207 338-1975
mikeh@midcoast.com
Photography: Belfast Bearfest™

MARYLAND

BALTIMORE

Fish Out of Water
www.aqua.org
National Aquarium in Baltimore
Volunteer Services
501 East Pratt Street Pier 3
Baltimore MD 21202
Contact: Leslie Landsman
410 576-1015
llandsman@aqua.org
Photography: Pat Venturino

MICHIGAN

BRIGHTON, FOWLERVILLE, HOWELL AND PINCKNEY

Animal House Fundraiser
Bear Necessities
www.livingstonhabitat.org
Livingston County Habitat for Humanity
7198 Grand River Road
Brighton MI 48114-7329
Contact: Jeff Doyle
810 220-9986
lchfh@sbcglobal.net
Photography: Jeff Doyle

GROSSE POINTE

Frogs•Fur•Friends
www.frogsfurfriends.org
C/O Budco
13700 Oakland Avenue
Highland Park MI 48203
Contact: Donna Brian
313 404-0020
donna@donnabrian.com
Photography: Jessica McCartney and Valerie White

ROCHESTER

The Ewe Revue
www.downtownrochestermi.com
Rochester DDA
308 ½ Main Street
Rochester MI 48307
Contact: Kristina K. Trevarrow
248 656-0060
dda@downtownrochestermi.com
Photography: Mitch Warde

MINNESOTA

ST. PAUL

St. Paul's Tribute to Charles M. Schulz
www.capitalcitypartnership.com
Capital City Partnership
2490 Wells Fargo Place 30 East 7th St.
St. Paul MN 55101
Contact: Sue Gonsior
651 291-5605
Photography: Bob Cole Photography; Tim Steinberg/Think Visuals Photo; Aaron Smith/Smitty's Workshop

MISSISSIPPI

MERIDIAN

Around Town
Carousels Abound
www.hopevillagems.org
2202 24th Street
Meridian MS 39302
Contact: Terri Province
601 553-8660
tprovince@hopevillagems.org
Photography: Shayne Garrett

MISSOURI

ST. LOUIS

The People Project
www.art-stl.com.com
St. Louis Regional Arts Commission
6128 Delmar Blvd
St. Louis MO 63112
Contact: Jill McGuire
314 863-5811
jill@stlrac.org
Photography: James Leick, Tony Schanuel and Brian Hall

NEBRASKA

KEARNEY

Cranes On Parade
www.cranesonparade.com
P.O. Box 2584
Kearney NE 68848
Contact: Julie Bray
2007 Chairperson
Scott McLaughlin
Public Relations
308 698-2228
info@cranesonparade.com
Photography: Scott McLaughlin and Patty Geist

NEVADA

RENO

Chair-i-ty
www.library.unr.edu/friends
2915 Solari Drive
Reno NV 89509
Contact: Michele Basta
775 827-6345
basta@unr.edu
Photography: Chair-i-ty

NEW HAMPSHIRE

North Hampton

Lighthouse LobStars
www.lighthousekids.org
Lighthouse Kids
39 Hobbs Road
North Hampton NH 03862
Contact: Jennifer King
603 964-6986
Susan Reynolds
603 978-2097
king.jen@comcast.net
Photography: Kristen Rand and Bill Lane

NEW MEXICO

Santa Fe

The Trail of Painted Ponies Inc.
www.trailofpaintedponies.com
P.O. Box 2629
Carefree AZ 85377-2629
Contact: Bryn Wilkins/
Karlynn Keyes
480 459-5700
Bryn@trailofpaintedponies.com
Karlynn@trailofpaintedponies.com
Photography: Eduardo Fuss, Don Bell and Bryn Wilkins at The Trail of Painted Ponies

NEW YORK

Buffalo

Herd About Buffalo™
www.buffalo.com
Roswell Park Cancer Institute
Elm & Calton Streets
Buffalo NY 14263
Contact: Monique Watts
716 845-8788
monique.watts@roswellpark.org
Photography: Ben Richey

New York

DOGNY® America's Tribute to Search & Rescue Dogs
www.akc.org
The American Kennel Club
260 Madison Ave.
4th Floor
New York NY 10016
Contact: Daphna Straus
dxs@akc.org
Ariela Schulman
ajs@akc.org
212 696-8200
Photography: Mary Spano and Paul Bereswill

NORTH CAROLINA

Charlotte

Chairs on Parade
www.mccollcenter.org
721 North Tyron Street
Charlotte NC 28202
Contact: John Turner
704 332-5535
jturner@mccollcenter.org
Photography: Karey C. Williams

NORTH DAKOTA

Grand Forks

UnFORKettable Art
www.visitgrandforks.com
211 South 4th Street
Grand Forks ND 58201
Contact: Edie Dahlen
701 746-0405
edie@cviconline.org
Contact: Barbara Kramer
Director Healthy Families Region IV
412 Demers Ave.
Grand Forks ND 58201
701 746-2064
Photography: Edie Dahlen

OHIO

Cincinnati

The Big Pig Gig™
A project of ArtWorks
www.ArtWorksCincinnati.org
Artworks
811 Race Street
Cincinnati OH 45202
Contact: Tamara Harkavy
513 333-0388
artworks@fuse.net
Photography: Javier Jarren

Cleveland

GuitarMania®
www.cleveland.com/guitarmania
United Way of Greater Cleveland
1331 Euclid Avenue
Cleveland OH 44115
Contact: Michelle Battle
216 436-2121
mbattle@uws.org
Photography: GuitarMania®

OKLAHOMA

Oklahoma City

Spirit of the Buffalo
www.spiritofthebuffalo.org
Contact: Juliette Hulen
405 607-2812
jujuhulen@yahoo.com
Photography: Tinker Hulen and Linda Barry

OREGON

Eugene

Ducks on Parade
www.downtowneugene.com
Downtown Eugene Inc.
132 East Broadway Suite 103
Eugene OR 97401
Contact: Michelle M. Emmons
Marketing Consultant
541 913-5718
michelle@downtowneugene.com
Photography: Linda and Steve Wheatley, Michelle Emmons and Janice Gould

Grants Pass

Grants Pass "BearFest"
www.bearfest.com
Evergreen Federal Bank
969 SE Sixth St.
Grants Pass OR 97526
Contact: Al Devine
Vice President Marketing
541 479-3351
ad@evergreenbanking.com
Photography: Grants Pass "BearFest"

Salem

Salmon in the City
www.salmoninthecity.com
Salmon in the City
P.O. Box 993
Salem Oregon 97308
Contact: Krina Lemons, Chair
503 932-3201
krinalemons@msn.com
Photography: Kelly James

PENNSYLVANIA

Erie

GoFish!© LeapFrog!
www.leapfrogerie.com
337 West 10th
Erie PA 16502
Contact: Jody Farrell
814 871-4100
jody@atomic74.com
Photography: Denis Kiem

RHODE ISLAND

Pawtucket

Blackstone Valley Canoe Trail
www.blackstonecanoetrail.com
Blackstone Valley Visitor Center
175 Main Street
Pawtucket RI 02860
Contact: Dr. Robert D. Billington / Lesley McLaughlin
401 724-2200
BVRI@aol.com
Photography: Bruce Gannon, Neville Lassotovitch, Jennifer MacGray, Lesley McLaughlin, Chris Nichols and Susan Wolfenden, and many more...

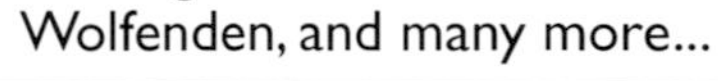

SOUTH CAROLINA

Myrtle Beach

Carousel Horses on Parade
www.RivoliTheatreGroup.com
3405 North Kings Hwy
Myrtle Beach SC 29577
Contact: Rachel Broadhurst
843 448-7169
Rachel@century21broadhurst.com
Photography: Anne Malarich

SOUTH DAKOTA

Custer

Custer Stampede
www.custerstampede.com
441 Mount Rushmore Road
Custer SD 57730
Contact: Toni Devereaux
605 673-5161
toni@rapidnet.com
Photography: Paul Horsted

TENNESSEE

Nashville

Nashville's GuitarTown Project
www.gibson.com
The Gibson Foundation
309 Plus Park Blvd.
Nashville TN 37217
Contact: Isla Waters
Manager, Events & GuitarTown
615 871-4500
isla.waters@gibson.com
Photography: Sandy Campbell
and Dean Dixon

TEXAS

Dallas

Dallas Soars!
Office of Cultural Affairs
1925 Elm Street Suite 400
Majestic Theatre
Dallas TX 75201
Contact: Margaret Robinette
214 670-3284
mrobine@mail.ci.dallas.tx.us
Photography: Shawn Northcutt
and Miguel Casanova

El Paso

Art and Sol
www.artandsolelpaso.org
Impact Programs of Excellence
444 East Robinson Suite B
El Paso TX 79902
Contact: Sally Gilbert/
Norma Geller
915 545-5068
impactprograms@hotmail.com
Photography: Art and Sol

Plainview

Plainview Cattle Drive
www.ci.plainview.tx.us
City of Plainview
901 Broadway
Plainview TX 79072
Contact: Eric Turner
806 296-1119
eturner@ci.plainview.tx.us
Photography: Plainview Cattle Drive

UTAH

Salt Lake City

Seagull Fest
www.seagullfest.org
824 South 700 East
Salt Lake City UT 84102
Contact: Renee Shaw
801 364-0607
avenues4artz@hotmail.com
Photography: Alisa Quist
and Colette Merril

Box Elder, Davis, Salt Lake, Summit, Wasatch and Weber County

The Utah Buffalo Round-up
www.utahbuffaloroundup.com
486 South 1400 East
Fruit Heights UT 84037
Contact: Rick Mayfield
801 593-6663
rjmayfield@msn.com
Photography: Robert Casey
and Jacom Stephens

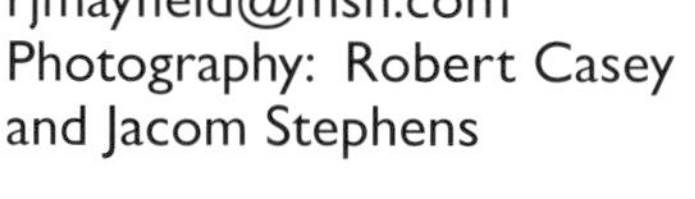

VERMONT

Ludlow

Llamas of Lludlow
www.lludlowllamas.com
119 Main Street
Ludlow VT 05149
Contact: Amber Nye
802 228-4703
llamas@tds.net
Photography: Amber Nye,
William Nye and Donald Dill

Manchester

A Horse Affair
www.ahorseaffair.com
5046 Main Street Suite 1
Manchester Center VT 05255
Contact: Jay Hathaway
802 362-6313
customer@manchesterchamber.net
Photography: Lee Krohn

VIRGINIA

Fredericksburg

Pawsitively Fredericksburg!
www.visitFred.com
110 Old Landing
Fredericksburg VA 22405
Contact: Sue Henderson
800 678-4748
suehenderson@earthlink.net
Photography: Rick Henderson,
Sue Henderson and Vince Staley

Norfolk

Mermaids On Parade
www.norfolk.gov
810 Union Street 302
Norfolk VA 23510
Contact: Bob Batcher
Public Relations Manager
757 664-4008
bob.batcher@norfolk.gov
Photography: Will Bassett

Winchester and Frederick County

Apples On Parade
www.winchesterva.org
Top of Virginia Regional Chamber
2 North Cameron Street
Suite 200
Winchester VA 22601
Contact: Jody Wall
540 662-4118
jwall@regionalchamber.biz
Photography: Lori M. Bridgeforth
Full Frame Photography

WASHINGTON

Seattle

Pigs On Parade
www.pigsonparade.org
Pike Place Market Foundation
85 Pike Street #550
Seattle WA 98101
Contact: Marlys Erickson
206 774-5246
marlys@pikeplacemarket.org
Photography: Corky Trewin at Puget
Sound Digital, Serge Timacheff
and David Perry

WASHINGTON

Bellevue, Leavenworth, Mount Vernon, Olympia, Orcas Island, Port Angeles, Port Townsend, Seattle and Tacoma

Soul Salmon
www.soulsalmon.org
P.O. Box 295
Chimacum WA 98325
Contact: Sara M. Johani
360 732-4238
housojay@olympus.net
Photography: Craig Wester, Sara Mall Johani, Frank Ross and Marty Peckman

WISCONSIN

Eau Claire

Hands Across Eau Claire
www.cmec.cc
220 South Barstow
Eau Claire WI 54701
Contact: Delana Nelson
715 835-7045
delnelsen@charter.net
Photography: Hands Across Eau Claire

Milwaukee

Beastie Beat™
www.mso.org
Milwaukee Symphony Orchestra League
9240 North Tennyson Drive
Bayside WI 53217
Contact: Bunny Raasch-Hooten
414 352-8802
brh@wi.rr.com
Photography: Rick Brodzeller

Racine

Dog Days of Summer
Cat'n Around Downtown
Downtown Bears It All
Downtown Summer Splash
www.racinepublicart.com
413 Main Street
Racine WI 53403
Contact: Terry Leopold
Special Events Director
262 898-2992
tleopold@racinedowntown.com
Photography: Brad Jaeck and Carol Hansen

WYOMING

Cheyenne

These Boots are made for Talking
www.cheyennedepotmuseum.org
Cheyenne Depot Museum Foundation
One Depot Square
121 West 15th Street Suite 301
Cheyenne WY 82001
Contact: Gordon G. Horton
307 637-3376
mail@cheyennedepotmuseumfoundation.org
Photography: Craig Maars Photography

RESOURCES

American ArtParades, LLC
www.americanartparades.com
P.O. Box 2629
Carefree AZ 85377-2629
Contact: Bryn Wilkins
480 459-5700
info@americanartparades.com

Business Here (Branded Online Auctions)
www.businesshere.com
Contact: Jonathan Skardon
937 222-7525
info@businesshere.com

Cowpainters LLC
www.cowpainters.com
811 West Evergreen Ave
Suite 110
Chicago IL 60622
312 666-6257
info@cowpainters.com

Fiberglass Farm
www.fiberglassfarm.com
93 Main Street
Belfast ME 04915
Contact: Mike Hurley
1 800 545-8956
207 338-1975
mikeh@midcoast.com

Icon Poly (City Art Projects)
www.iconpolystudio.com
150 Odessa Rd.
Odessa NE 68861
308 234-9411
info@iconpolystudio.com

TIVOLITOO, Inc.
www.tivolitoo.com
2444 Enterprise Drive
Suite A
Mendota Heights MN 55120
Contact: Hart Johnson
651 698-3335
hartj@tivolitoo.com

The Trail of Painted Ponies, Inc.
www.trailofpaintedponies.com
P.O. Box 2629
Carefree AZ 85377-2629
Contact: Rod Barker
480 459-5700
info@trailofpaintedponies.com

Glossary of Art Terms

The following art terms are defined as they relate to ***American ArtParades***:

American ArtParades Outdoor Public Art Projects featuring large fiberglass sculptures of cultural or animal icons, painted and decorated by regional artists and exhibited throughout cities, sponsored by local businesses and individuals and auctioned after the exhibitions, with the proceeds benefiting designated non-profit organizations. Innovative business model for cultural partnerships between artists, non-profits, businesses and tourism bureaus. New American Art Movement.

Abstract Art Art that departs significantly from natural appearances. Forms are modified or changed to varying degrees in order to emphasize certain qualities or content.

Abstract Expressionism An art movement, primarily in painting, that originated in the United States in the 1940s and remained strong through the 1950s. Artists working in many different styles emphasized spontaneous personal expression.

Acrylic (acrylic resin) A clear plastic used as a binder in paint and as a casting material in sculpture.

Action Painting A style of nonrepresentational painting that relies on the physical movement of the artist in using such gestural techniques as vigorous brushwork, dripping, and pouring.

Additive Color Mixture When light colors are combined, the result becomes successively lighter. Light primaries, when combined, create white light. See also subtractive color mixture.

Additive Sculpture Sculptural form produced by combining or building up material from a core or armature. Modeling in clay and welding steel are additive processes.

Aesthetics The study and philosophy of the quality and nature of sensory responses related to, but not limited by, the concept of beauty.

Airbrush A small-scale paint sprayer that allows the artist to control a fine mist of paint.

Analogous Colors Closely related hues, especially those in which we can see a common hue; hues that are neighbors on the color wheel, such as blue, blue-green, and green.

Applied Art Art in which aesthetic values are used in the design or decoration of utilitarian objects.

Assemblage Sculpture using preexisting, sometimes "found" objects that may or may not contribute their original identities to the total content of the work.

Asymmetrical Without symmetry. Unbalanced.

Avant-garde French for advance guard" or "vanguard." Those considered the leaders (and often regarded as radicals) in the invention and application of new concepts in a given field.

Axis An implied straight line in the center of a form along its dominant direction.

Balance An arrangement of parts achieving a state of equilibrium between opposing forces or influences. Major types are symmetrical and asymmetrical.

Beneficiary The organization that received the proceeds from the sales and auctions of works of art from American ArtParades.

Curvilinear Formed or characterized by curving lines or edges.

Binder The material used in paint that causes pigment particles to adhere to one another and to the support; for example, linseed oil or acrylic polymer.

Carving A subtractive process in which a sculpture is formed by removing material from a block or mass of wood, stone, or other material, using sharpened tools.

Casting A process that involves pouring liquid material such as molten metal, clay, wax, or plaster into a mold. When the liquid hardens, the mold is removed, leaving a form in the shape of the mold.

Ceramic Objects made of clay hardened into a relatively permanent material by firing. Also, the process of making such objects.

Chiaroscuro Italian for "light-dark." The gradations of light and dark values in two-dimensional imagery; especially the illusion of rounded, three-dimensional form created through gradations of light and shade rather than line.

Collage From the French coller, to glue. A work made by gluing materials such as paper scraps, photographs, and cloth on to a flat surface.

Color Field Painting A movement that grew out of Abstract Expressionism, in which large stained or painted areas or "fields of color evoke aesthetic and emotional responses.

Color Wheel A circular arrangement of contiguous spectral hues used in some color systems. Also called a color circle.

Complementary Colors Two hues directly opposite one another on a color wheel which, when mixed together in proper proportions, produce a neutral gray.

Composition The bringing together of parts or elements to form a whole; the structure, organization, or total form of a work of art.

Contour The edge or apparent line that separates one area or mass from another; a line following a surface drawn to suggest volume.

Contrapposto The counterpositioning of parts of the human figure about a central vertical axis, as when the weight is placed on one foot, causing the hip and shoulder lines to counterbalance each other, often in a graceful S-curve.

Cool Colors Colors whose relative visual temperatures make them seem cool. Cool colors generally include green, blue-green, blue, blue-violet, and violet. The quality of warmness or coolness is relative to adjacent hues.

Cubism Cubism is based on the simultaneous presentation of multiple views, disintegration, and the geometric reconstruction of objects in flattened, ambiguous pictorial so space.

Eclecticism The practice of selecting or borrowing from earlier styles and combining the borrowed elements.

Edition A limited number of multiple originals of a single design in any medium.

Encaustic A painting medium in which pigment is suspended in a binder of hot wax.

Expressionism The broad term that describes emotional art, most often boldly executed and making free use of distortion and symbolic or invented color.

Eye Level The height of the viewer's eyes above the ground plane.

Figure Separate shape(s) distinguishable from a background or ground.

Fine Art Art created for purely aesthetic expression, communication, or contemplation. Painting and sculpture are the best known of the fine arts.

Folk Art Art of people who have had no formal, academic training, but whose works are part of an established tradition of style and craftsmanship.

Foreshortening The representation of forms on a two-dimensional surface by presenting the length in such a way that the long axis appears to project toward or recede away from the viewer.

Form In the broadest sense, the total physical characteristics of an object.

Formalist Having an emphasis on highly structured visual relationships rather than on subject matter or nonvisual content.

Format The shape or proportions of a picture plane.

Frontal An adjective describing an object that faces the viewer directly, rather than being set at an angle or foreshortened.

Gesso A mixture of glue and either chalk or plaster of Paris applied as a ground or coating to surfaces in order to give them the correct properties to receive paint.

Glaze In oil painting, a thin transparent or translucent layer brushed over another layer of paint, allowing the first layer to show through but altering its color slightly.

Gothic Primarily an architectural style that prevailed in western Europe from the 20th through the 15th centuries, characterized by pointed arches, ribbed vaults, and flying buttresses, that made it possible to create stone buildings that reached great heights.

Gouache An opaque, water-soluble paint. Watercolor to which opaque white has been added.

Happening An event conceived by artists and performed by artists and others, usually unrehearsed and without a specific script or stage.

Hard-edge A term first used in the 1950s to distinguish styles of painting in which shapes are precisely defined by sharp edges, in contrast to the usually blurred or soft edges in Abstract Expressionist paintings.

Horizon Line In linear perspective, the implied or actual line or edge placed on a two- dimensional surface to represent the place in nature where the sky meets the horizontal land or water plane.

Hue That property of a color identifying a specific, named wavelength of light such as green, red, violet, and so on.

Icon An image or symbolic representation often with very important or sacred significance.

Impasto In painting, thick paint applied to a surface in a heavy manner, having the appearance and consistency of buttery paste.

Impressionism A style of painting that originated in France about 1870. Paintings of casual subjects, executed outdoors, using divided brush strokes to capture the mood of a particular moment as defined by the transitory effects of light and color.

Intensity The relative purity or saturation of a hue (color), on a scale from bright (pure) to dull (mixed with another hue or a neutral. Also called chroma.

Intermediate Color A hue between a primary and a secondary on the color wheel, such as yellow-green, a mixture of yellow and green.

Kinetic Art Art that incorporates actual movement as part of the design.

Local Color The actual color as distinguished from the apparent color of objects and surfaces; true color, without shadows or reflections.

Logo Sign, name, or trademark of an organization, institution, firm, or publication, consisting of letter forms borne on one printing plate or piece of type.

Low Key Consistent use of dark values within a given area or surface.

Lumina The use of actual light as an art medium.

Mass Three-dimensional form having physical bulk. Also, the illusion of such a form on a two-dimensional surface.

Matte A dull finish or surface, especially in sculpture, painting, photography, and ceramics.

Medium A particular material along with its accompanying technique; a specific type of artistic technique or means of expression determined by the use of particular materials.

Minimalism A nonrepresentational style from the 1960's; usually severely restricted in the use of visual elements and often consisting of simple geometric shapes or masses.

Mixed Media Works of art made with more than one medium.

Mobile A type of sculpture in which parts move, often activated by air currents.

Modeling 1. Working pliable material such as clay or wax into three-dimensional forms. 2. In drawing or painting, the effect of light falling on a three-dimensional object so that the illusion of its mass is created and defined by value gradations.

Modernism Theory and practice in late 19th and 20th century art, which holds that each new generation must build on past styles in new ways or break with the past in order to make the next major historical contribution.

Monochromatic A color scheme limited to variations of one hue, a hue with its tints and/or shades.

Montage A composition made up of pictures or parts of pictures previously drawn, painted, or photographed.

Mosaic An art medium in which small pieces of colored glass, stone, or ceramic tile called tessera are embedded in a background material such as plaster or mortar. Also, works made using this technique.

Naturalism Representational art in which the artist presents a subjective interpretation of visual reality while retaining something of the natural appearance or look of the objects depicted.

Naive Art Art made by people with no formal art training.

Negative Shape A background or ground shape seen in relation to foreground or figure shapes.

Neutrals Not associated with any single hue. Blacks, whites, grays, and dull gray-browns. A neutral can be made by mixing complementary hues.

Non-profits Also known as not-for-profits, are organizations whose primary objective is dedicated to the greater good and not for financial gain. These include animal, environmental, educational, artistic and health related organizations.

Nonrepresentational Art without reference to anything outside itself-without representation. Also called nonobjective-without recognizable objects.

Oil Paint Paint in which the pigment is held together with a binder of oil, usually linseed oil.

Opaque Impenetrable by light; not transparent or translucent.

Painterly Painting characterized by openness of form, in which shapes are defined by loose brushwork in light and dark color areas rather than by outline or contour.

Pastels 1. Sticks of powdered pigment held together with a gum binding agent. 2. Pale colors or tints.

Perspective A system for creating an illusion of depth or three-dimensional space on a two-dimensional surface.

Pictorial Space In a painting or other two-dimensional art, illusionary space which appears to recede backward into depth from the picture plane.

Pigment Any coloring agent, made from natural or synthetic substances, used in paints or drawing materials.

Plastic 1. Pliable; capable of being shaped. Pertaining to the process of shaping or modeling (i.e., the plastic arts). 2. Synthetic polymer substances, such as acrylic.

Pointillism A system of painting using tiny dots or "points" of color, developed by French artist Georges Seurat in the 1880s.

Polychromatic Having many colors; random or intuitive use of color combinations as opposed to color selection based on a specific color scheme.

Pop Art A style of painting and sculpture that developed in the late 1950s and early 1960s, based on the visual subject matter, and impersonal style of popular mass-media imagery.

Positive Shape A figure or foreground shape, as opposed to a negative ground or background shape.

Post-Modern In the visual arts, it is characterized by an acceptance of all periods and styles, including modernism, and a willingness to combine elements of all styles and periods.

Prehistoric Art Art created before written history, often the only record of early cultures.

Primary Colors Those hues that cannot be produced by mixing other hues. Pigment primaries are red, yellow, and blue.

Prime In painting, a first layer of paint or sizing applied to a surface that is to be painted.

Proportion The size relationship of parts to a whole and to one another.

Public Art Works of art created for the enjoyment of the general public and placed in outdoor and indoor public spaces.

Realism A type of representational art in which the artist depicts as closely as possible what the eye sees. Based on the idea that ordinary people and everyday activities are worthy subjects for art.

Relief Sculpture Sculpture in which three-dimensional forms project from a flat background of which they are a part. The degree of projection can vary and is described by the terms high relief and low relief.

Representational Art Art in which it is the artist's intention to present again or represent a particular subject; especially pertaining to realistic portrayal of subject matter.

Reproduction A mechanically produced copy of an original work of art; not to be confused with an original sculpture or art print.

Rhythm The regular or ordered repetition of dominant and subordinate elements or units within a design.

Scale The size or apparent size of an object seen in relation to other objects, people, or its environment.

Sculpture A three dimensional work of art cast in a poly-resin.

Secondary Colors Pigment secondaries are the hues orange, violet, and green, which may be produced in slightly dulled form by mixing two primaries.

Shade A hue with black added.

Shape A two-dimensional or implied two-dimensional area defined by line or changes in value and/or color.

Simultaneous Contrast An optical effect caused by the tendency of contrasting forms and colors to emphasize their difference when they are placed together.

Site-specific Art Any work made for a certain place, which cannot be separated or exhibited apart from its intended environment.

Size Any of several substances made from glue, wax, or clay, used as a filler for porous material such as paper, canvas or other cloth, or wall surfaces. Used to protect the surface from the deteriorating effects of paint.

Sponsor Individuals and organizations that paid to sponsor or support an artist or work of art for American ArtParades.

Still Life A painting or other two-dimensional work of art representing inanimate objects such as bottles, fruit, and flowers. Also, the arrangement of these objects from which a drawing, painting, or other work is made.

Style A characteristic handling of media and elements of form that gives a work its identity as the product of a particular person, group, art movement, period, or culture.

Stylized Simplified or exaggerated visual form which emphasizes particular or contrived design qualities.

Subtractive Sculpture Sculpture made by removing material from a larger block or form.

Support The physical material that provides the base for and sustains a two-dimensional work of art. Metal of rebar is used to support many sculptural forms.

Symbol A form or image implying or representing something beyond its obvious meaning.

Symmetry A design (or composition) with identical or nearly identical form on opposite sides of a dividing line or central axis; formal balance.

Tempera A water-based paint that uses egg, egg yolk, glue, or casein as a binder. Many commercially made paints identified as tempera are actually gouache.

Tessera Bit of colored glass, ceramic tile, or stone used in a mosaic.

Texture The tactile quality of a surface or the representation or invention of the appearance of such a surface quality.

Three-dimensional Having height, width, and depth.

Tint A hue with white added.

Tompe l'oeil French for "fool the eye." A two-dimensional representation that is so naturalistic that it looks actual or real (three-dimensional.)

Two-dimensional Having the dimensions of height and width only.

Unity The appearance of similarity, consistency, or oneness. Interrelational factors that cause various elements to appear as part of a single complete form.

Value The lightness or darkness of tones or colors. White is the lightest value; black is the darkest. The value halfway between these extremes is called middle gray.

Vanishing Point In linear perspective, the point on the horizon line at which lines or edges that are parallel appear to converge.

Vehicle Liquid emulsion used as a carrier or spreading agent in paints.

Visualize To form a mental image or vision; to imagine.

Volume 1. Space enclosed or filled by a three-dimensional object or figure. 2. The implied space filled by a painted or drawn object or figure. Synonym: mass.

Warm Colors Colors whose relative visual temperature makes them seem warm. Warm colors or hues include red-violet, red, red-orange, orange, yellow-orange, and yellow.

Wash A thin, transparent layer of paint or ink.

Watercolor Paint that uses water-soluble gum as the binder and water as the vehicle, characterized by transparency.

Edited from the Glossary provided by the Ackland Art Museum, www.ackland.org.

Autographs

www.AmericanArtParades.com

A HORSE *Affair*
Manchester Center, Vermont

Adopt-A-Bee
Zion, Illinois

Animal House FUNDRAISER
Howell, Michigan

The Bear Necessities FUNDRAISER
Howell, Michigan

BEASTIE BEAT™
Milwaukee, Wisconsin

Belfast Bearfest
Belfast, Maine

THE BIG PIG GIG™
Cincinnati, Ohio

Chairs On Parade
Charlotte, North Carolina

CHARLIE BROWN AROUND TOWN
St. Paul, Minnesota

Cows on Parade™ In Chicago
Chicago, Illinois

COOL CITY CARS
Wilmington, Delaware

Dallas Soars!
Dallas, Texas

DINO DAYS
Wilmington, Delaware

DISCOVERY DOG
Sioux City, Iowa

Dog Days of Summer
Racine, Wisconsin

Downtown Bears It All
Racine, Wisconsin

Downtown Summer Splash
Racine, Wisconsin

DUCKS ON PARADE
Eugene, Oregon

THE EWE REVUE
Rochester, Michigan

gators ON THE geaux
Lake Charles, Louisiana

Geckos in Paradise SM
Honolulu, Hawaii

GEESE GALORE
Longmont, Colorado

Go Fish!©
Erie, Pennsylvania

HERD ABOUT BUFFALO™
Buffalo, New York

Leap Frog!
Erie, Pennsylvania

Lighthouse LobStars
North Hampton, New Hampshire

LINUS BLANKETS SAINT PAUL
St. Paul, Minnesota

MASTODONS ON PARADE
Fort Wayne, Indiana

Mermaids On Parade
Norfolk, Virginia

Nashville's GuitarTown
Nashville, Tennessee

NO MOOSE Left Behind
Coeur d'Alene, Idaho

Pawsitively Fredericksburg!
Fredericksburg, Virginia

PEANUTS ON PARADE
St. Paul, Minnesota

Peanuts Around Town
Dothan, Alabama

THE PEOPLE PROJECT
St. Louis, Missouri

SALMON IN THE CITY
Salem, Oregon

Seagull Fest
Salt Lake City, Utah

SHARKBYTE ART™
San Jose, California

SOUL SALMON
Washington

Trout About Downtown
San Luis Obispo, California

Tybee Turtle Tour
Tybee Island, Georgia

UnFORKettable ART
Grand Forks, North Dakota

Urban Trees
San Diego, California